MY LIFE CHANGED FOREVER

The Years I Have Lost as a
Target of Organized Stalking

BY

ELIZABETH SULLIVAN

INFINITY
PUBLISHING.COM

ISBN 978-0-7414-4920-7

Published by:

INFINITY
PUBLISHING.COM

1094 New DeHaven Street, Suite 100
West Conshohocken, PA 19428-2713
Info@buybooksontheweb.com
www.buybooksontheweb.com
Toll-free (877) BUY BOOK
Local Phone (610) 941-9999
Fax (610) 941-9959

Printed in the United States of America

Published October 2012

CONTENTS

INTRODUCTION

Can you imagine living a fairly normal and average life in the suburbs and one day awakening to the fact that you are suddenly under constant surveillance, no matter where you are? Can you imagine the frustration of knowing this is true and that you are of sound mind, and yet what is happening is so bizarre that you don't even know how to describe it without sounding delusional? This is the life I have been living since 1994.

Since 1994, I have been the target of something known as "group stalking" or "organized stalking." It is a crime of hate and control by a large group of people. Indeed, it is a form of organized crime. This is a story that may be very hard to believe, but it is actually happening to me and to many others around the country. This book is a true story about being targeted and stalked by a deceitful and mean-spirited person (the lead perpetrator) and a very large group of people (the group members). They would all have to be considered unstable sociopaths at the very least. It is a story of being under constant surveillance.

This elaborate "game" has caused much turmoil, stress and frustration in my life, and I am not the same person I was before it started. In many ways, I have lost the years of my life since this started. The changes in me did not happen overnight. It has been a slow process as my family's privacy has been invaded over and over and over. Prior to 1994, I would have described myself as a very trusting, happy, and optimistic person. I was friendly and smiled often. I enjoyed meeting new people and being around friends and family.

Now, after so many long years of this, I have become suspicious of strangers, and sometimes even acquaintances. At times, I have found myself not returning a person's smile because I think they might be a participant in this intrusive, horrible game. To know you have done nothing and yet to feel a sort of dislike and disrespect from complete strangers is a very uncomfortable feeling. I honestly fear for my life, my health and my safety on a daily basis. How can I possibly know of what these serial stalkers are capable? They have acted in an illegal and immoral manner since 1994.

Names and locations mentioned in the book have been changed or disguised for the protection of my family only. I don't care at all about protecting the identities of the stalkers, but by changing their names, I am protecting myself, also. I will also not reveal identifying information such as our professions, employers, or any identifying information about our daughter. I will not reveal most conversations I have had with private investigators or law enforcement personnel. One person I believe to be behind this is a medical doctor by the name of Anthony Hanson, M.D. The latest information I have, which is from several years ago, is that he works and resides in City X. I am not sure in what capacity he is still involved, but I am almost sure that he, or someone from his office, was instrumental in starting the organized stalking activities in 1994 in City A. I am hoping that by documenting the story, I may eventually get some answers.

As I will disclose in this book, the people who found ways to break into our homes, presumably to install and tend to hidden surveillance equipment and to snoop into our computers and other personal items, had little respect for our home or our belongings.

Over the course of the many years this has been going on, we have had walls and ceilings nicked and scratched, holes punched in our drywall, light fixtures broken, a window broken, locks tampered with, weather stripping cut, lamp and chandelier fixture sockets loosened and even replaced, a ceramic tile chipped, furniture scratched and banged up, doors and door thresholds gouged and scratched, appliances tampered with and broken, a hole punched through our exterior stucco, and many, many more things damaged.

As long as this has been going on, it has been hard to come up with proof, other than all of the damage and strange, ridiculous things that have happened to our cars, our houses, our telephones, our computers, and my family. The people involved seem much more interested in continuing their game, at any cost, than in giving any thought as to how it is affecting us. In fact, it is a reaction and acknowledgement from the target that excites the stalkers and keeps them going. Experts advise stalking victims not to react or get upset in front of the stalkers, but that is sometimes difficult!

Over the years, I have written pages and pages of notes documenting many of the strange events that have happened. These are not nearly all of the stalking-related events, as this has gone on 24/7/365 since at least 1994, but these are some of the events that I took the time to document. It is from all of these notes, and my recollections, that this book is written. All of the years that this has been going on have been filled, over and over and over, with the same sorts of things that are documented here. This book will barely scratch the surface on the subject of organized stalking.

As I will write about later in the book, it was not until 2003 that I became aware of the concept of organized stalking. The stalking went on for nine years before I knew it had a name! That answered many questions about the organized and systematic way in which we have been treated, but not about who did it or why. It would be easy to isolate any one (or two or three) of the incidents I write about and say that they could happen to anyone. That is very true. However, when the same sorts of things happen hundreds or thousands of times to one person, it becomes less and less likely that the same things could randomly happen to everyone.

Although this horrible game has gone on for years, I still have no definite answers. I do have a theory. My theory is that there is an elaborate Internet and cell phone based stalking game, which involves a large number of people. I think they have placed transmitting devices, and probably cameras, in our houses, and our cars and telephones have been bugged, also. I believe Anthony Hanson was involved, at least in the beginning, and probably all along. It is probable that there is a website detailing our lives and whereabouts at all times. It is possible that webcams, our phone calls, and even our online computer use are connected to this site. There are obviously people involved in this who are knowledgeable about technology and surveillance tactics. Some of these people were no doubt recruited into organized stalking for that knowledge.

For most of the initial years the stalking was going on, I always assumed that no one would want a person (the target) to know they were being stalked.

Even after I realized this was organized stalking, I thought they wouldn't want us to know. I guess I was confusing them with "real" spies, like one sees on television or in the movies. It turns out I was wrong about that. Apparently, the instructions for group stalking members are not to get caught or identified and to make sure the targets know they ARE being watched and followed. That is part of their protocol.

I thought for a long time that they were really pathetic spies because they were so obvious. A car would pull out behind me and follow me for miles, even if I made a wrong turn. I not only found them disgusting, but it was ridiculous that they were so obvious! The same was true when I was being followed while walking. Well, for all these years, they have continued to try to make sure I DO notice them. Any attempt on their part to stop following me at various points probably had more to do with not wanting to be identified.

We are an ordinary family. My husband, Mark, and I have a daughter, Cindy, who was seven years old in 1994, when I believe all of this started. We were living in City A. We moved to City B in 1997 and to City C in 1999. Both moves were job related. The stalking has continued through the moves, in three different large cities in the United States. I believe it was probably a matter of being in the wrong place at the wrong time. For some unknown reason, it seemed to start after a routine visit to Dr. Anthony Hanson in early 1994, in City A.

Some of the suspected participants in all of this are Anthony Hanson, M.D., and a tall, slender woman, at least 5' 10" to 6 feet tall. On several occasions, she has been with another rather tall woman. I have seen these same people on several occasions, in different cities where I have been. They often have different looks (disguises), but I have seen some of the same people in different locations. If a connection can be found between Anthony Hanson and this tall woman and/or man, I believe some of the puzzle could be solved.

Maybe the connection is a colleague or former colleague, a relative, or a friend. Does he have any personal or professional connections to any of the Federal agencies? I have to allow for that possibility since I have no idea why I (we) have been targeted. That might also explain the ease with which the stalkers are able to intrude whenever they want and persuade others to cooperate with them. As I will discuss later, I believe Dr. Hanson's office had a hidden camera in the examining room. Who else saw what went on in the examining room? That could also be a key.

I reported everything to the FBI in City B in early 1999, and again in City C in 2003, using real names and locations. They were of no help. I think that a potential stalker should be taken very seriously. If this has gone on since 1994, I have no idea if it will ever end. Even if they were to eventually retreat for a while, they could come back into our lives as easily as they did in the past. As easily as they did each time we moved.

After all this time, I wonder what they might be capable of. What kind of person would do this? What kind of person would participate in such a game? What kind of person thinks so little of others' privacy that he would allow and encourage numerous strangers to listen to other people's private conversations? I believe he is a sociopath who has made a game of doing all of this without leaving any real proof. That must be the challenge for him. How could anyone think it is funny or justified to entertain others in this way? I think that they have used my life and my family for entertainment and perhaps even for profit and other motives.

I have become fearful because I don't know who is involved in this. Since there is a history of continual destruction to our belongings, I wonder what else might happen. If he becomes angry enough that I am on to him, or that I might expose him, I worry that he could try to hurt or assault me more than he already has. I worry about what he has already done to me. I need to find the truth about what has been going on all these years. I am hoping that someone who reads this book will recognize our situation and be willing to reveal what they know. Perhaps some tactic or event that we don't understand will mean something to someone else.

Also, in an effort to protect ourselves, I will not disclose certain details that could be of benefit to the stalkers. I will not give any details on the types of locks, security systems or surveillance equipment that we have or do not have. I do reveal some information about our past homes, but we have learned at least some things over the years. I will also not include any information or discoveries we have made over the years that we don't want the stalkers to know that we know.

Every time I suspected or was sure that an intruder had been in the house, I knew it was true. They have entered the house when all the doors and windows were locked and when the security system was armed. I don't have all the answers as to how they accomplished this, but I do know they have done it. It seems that the stalkers can be relentless if they really want to enter a target's home. I have come to the conclusion that if a person has enough money, connections, and persuasive skills, he will be able to enter a residence eventually.

I believe this has to do with the stalkers knowing how to bribe people and convince people to do something and knowing how to contact employees and ex-employees who will provide information or do what they need to have done. Basically, these are people without consciences. The same would be true for illegally breaking into someone else's vehicle or computer and illegally tapping someone else's telephone. I used to refer to these stalkers as "spy wannabes," but I have come to realize that they are really organized stalkers and torturers.

They have impersonated us when they broke in and stayed for periods of time in our houses while we were gone. They have intruded while we were sleeping. It appears that there are no details of our lives that they don't feel entitled to. They are obsessed, intrusive and self-serving.

I want to publish this book so I can tell my story. Even though I am writing it under a pseudonym, there may be a few people with whom I will share this book on a personal level. Not only am I a target of organized stalking, but I believe the people who were instrumental in starting the stalking are responsible for ruining my health and well being. I will describe in this book how I have awakened numerous times to see two men in the bedroom. I believe they have drugged me in order to use me as a test subject for illegal, unscrupulous and involuntary experimentation. I believe these two individuals have been involved in triggering or inducing some of the serious medical conditions I have developed over the past several years, since the stalking began.

I am basing this speculation on several facts. I was a healthy and happy woman before these atrocities began. All of my conditions and symptoms have been documented as possible results of technological harassment and torture, not to mention direct medical experimentation. I have distinct memories of seeing two men in my bedroom and of feeling woozy and drugged when I did awaken enough to see them. I have absolutely no family history of any of the health conditions I have developed. The organized stalking might have been a cover for the physical harassment, or the organized stalking may have escalated into physical attacks at a later time. The organized stalking began in 1994. I have recollections of feeling drugged and waking just enough to see two men in the room as early as 1995.

I know more than anyone how unbelievable this story sounds. That is one of the reasons I have been forced to keep it to myself for so long. However, I have come to realize that there are more evil people around than I would have ever believed. I do know that organized stalking exists.

Please see the appendixes for samples of some of the literature on organized stalking.

CHAPTER ONE

1994 – 1997: CITY A

In January of 1994, we lived in City A. We had lived there since 1991. I was having allergy symptoms and I called my doctor. She referred me to an allergy and immunology practice, and the receptionist said I would be seen by Dr. Anthony Hanson. When Dr. Hanson entered the exam room, I remember that he walked over to a table that had medical supplies on it and seemed to make a slight adjustment to something on the table. I didn't think too much about it – I just figured he must like things to be in their place. Dr. Hanson took my history, examined me, and suggested that I have skin testing to determine what allergies I might have.

The doctor told me the nurse would be coming in to start the skin testing, and he left the room so I could change into a gown. The nurse came in a few minutes later and was very pleasant and talkative. She was getting things set up when all of a sudden she seemed to see something that made her very angry. She stopped talking and started banging things around. I remember she opened the drawer of the table with medical supplies on it and slammed it shut hard. It was as if something had made her very angry and she was trying to make a point to someone. She excused herself from the room, and when she returned a few minutes later, she seemed to have calmed down. I have often asked myself why I didn't ask her what was wrong. All I can say is that for some reason, I decided to remain silent at that moment. If I had the chance to do it over again, I would have asked. However, my guess is that she might not have told me what made her so angry anyway.

As I have thought about it over the years, I have come to the conclusion that Dr. Hanson may have had a hidden camera in the room, and the nurse no doubt felt it was an invasion of privacy. It was probably what Dr. Hanson adjusted on the table, and probably what she noticed as she was setting up for the testing. Perhaps she realized that it had been on while I was getting undressed. I do remember that when Dr. Hanson was describing the skin testing, he assured me that they would be "checking on me" throughout the testing while they waited for reactions. However, no one ever came into the room during that time. Whether my hunch is correct or not doesn't change anything, but it might explain Dr. Hanson's interest in secretly watching people. I still wonder if that was the day that Dr. Hanson or someone else in the office decided that for whatever reason, I might be a possible subject or victim for whatever they were planning. I am just searching for answers.

Within a few weeks after that, my life began to change. Of all the hundreds and hundreds of strange things that have happened to me since then, there have been some common denominators: Dr. Anthony Hanson and at least two rather tall, slender women. The women have worn several different hairstyles and looks, but I believe they are the same women. Within a few weeks after my visit to his office, I started to hear a faint beep at the end of all my phone calls on my home phone. I have heard the same sort of beep on recorded phone messages, but I really had no idea of the significance of it. I just knew that I had never heard it before on our phone, and I would always hear it if I let the other person hung up first. The beep remained for the rest of the time we lived in City A, which was until 1997.

A few weeks after my appointment with Dr. Hanson, Mark and I happened to drive by the street corner where Dr. Hanson's office was. It was at a location that we drove by fairly often. It was early on a Saturday evening, and we had talked very specifically about where we were going and when we would leave home. With almost perfect timing, as we were driving by that corner, I saw Dr. Hanson turn out of his office parking lot. I didn't recognize his vehicle or anything, but I recognized him driving.

In late January or February, 1994, I remember talking to Mark at his office one evening after I had taken our daughter, Cindy, to her dance lesson. I mentioned the mall where her lesson was by name because I was telling Mark about something special that was going on there, how it was always empty on Monday nights but on that particular night it had been crowded. This particular mall was not a crowded or trendy mall. It was usually deserted on Monday nights, but I went there every Monday night because I took Cindy to her dance lesson.

One night, we were leaving dance class in February or March. It was a cold night, and Cindy and I were hurrying out to my van. I remember being a little perplexed because a security guard was escorting a man into the mall just as we were leaving. Then, when we got to my van, the front passenger door was unlocked! I never leave my car unlocked, so that was very unusual. After I got in and started the car, I saw a different man get out of the passenger side of a car parked a few spaces down, facing us. It was as if he had been waiting in the car. I had not noticed him before he got out of the car. He turned around once and looked at us, and then he headed toward the mall. I got the impression that the first man had come from the same car that this man got out of. What had the security guard found him doing, and why was my car unlocked when I was sure I had locked it?

The next week, I saw Dr. Anthony Hanson at the mall just as we arrived for Cindy's dance class. He was walking along slowly in front of the stores on the other side. A week or two later, I noticed a woman watching Cindy's dance class from the mall. I was sitting on one of the benches outside the studio. The dance studio had windows facing the mall side, and it was not unusual for people to stop for a few minutes and watch the dance classes. The woman that night seemed to watch for a long time – maybe 5 to 10 minutes. I looked across to the other side of the mall, and there was Dr. Hanson, standing in front of the stores on the other side. When he saw me looking at him, he started walking. It seemed like he was waiting for this woman who was watching the dance class. I never forgot her face because it was disturbing in a way, and I found out later that she was Anthony Hanson's wife! (She was not one of the tall women I referred to.) Was this all a coincidence, or did they know we would be there? What was going on?

From that point on, strange things continued to happen to me. There were so many that I started to document them because I had every intention of finding out what was going on. To this day, I still haven't. Not every incident I write about is necessarily related to the stalking, but they are all strange things that have happened since it started. The only theory I have is that I was in the wrong place at the wrong time, and my family and I have become the targets of an elaborate organized stalking game. What this has to do with Anthony Hanson and the tall women, I don't know, but I know they have continued to show up at places they couldn't possibly know about unless my phones were tapped, my home was bugged, and my car could be followed. There may be another mastermind behind this, but they are involved somehow. I have to believe that in order to involve the number of people that they have, they must have some extraordinary explanation of what they are doing. I believe they are sociopaths who enjoy playing mind games. Again, I need to say that we are ordinary people, and I have never been able to come up with a reason why we were selected as targets.

Around March of 1994, someone broke into our house in City A. Again, it was a Monday night, while I was at Cindy's dance lesson. They obviously already knew our Monday night routine and when we would be away from the house. Cindy and I had come directly home and we were both upstairs. Mark was working late at the office. I heard a door shut downstairs and I went to see what Cindy was up to, but she was still upstairs in her bedroom! I ran downstairs, but there was no sign of anything or anyone. I went out to the garage and found the pedestrian door unlocked, but nothing else was messed with. Then I noticed that the lock on the doorknob to the house was all scratched up as if it had been tampered with. I told Mark about it that night, and he said that his key had probably scratched it. He didn't want to believe that someone had broken into our house. I tried to forget about it since nothing was missing and I hadn't been able to find any other explanation. As I looked back on the incident later, I was fairly certain that it was how they got into our house the first time. We were not in the habit of locking the deadbolt on that door, and there was no security system on that house. All of the locks on our doors opened with the same key, and I kept several duplicates in a box on some bookshelves. If someone had broken in, they could have taken or made a duplicate of our house key.

I began to notice that my computer was being tampered with. I was definitely the only one using it; Cindy never went into my office, and Mark had his own computer. I noticed that the cords on the back of my computer were loosened and not in the same pattern. A lamp cord was now underneath all the other cords, and I knew it had been plugged in last, over all the others.

It was disturbing, and I knew these things could not happen by themselves. Next, several new printer icons showed up on my printer control panel screen. I had only placed my own printer icon on there, and now there were about ten. I was told that there was no way for printer icons to spontaneously appear; they had to have been installed one at a time. Also, all the fonts except one were deleted from my computer. Soon after that, my hard drive was completely wiped out by a computer virus. This was before the time when most people had some kind of security software on their computers.

At around that time, my neighbor from two houses away came over to visit one afternoon. She wanted to talk to me about something, and I remember that she was very specific. She asked if I was teaching a computer class or something because she had seen several women carrying computers into my house the previous Wednesday! I had no background in teaching computer classes, but that was what she assumed it was. She was sure of the time and sure of what she had seen, but it was an afternoon that I had not even been at home! She was even specific about where they parked. Why would those women bring computers into my house? I wanted to do something about it, but I didn't know what to do. I was still completely clueless. I now suspected that their visit was related to the new printer icons, the deleted fonts and the computer virus. Why would several women risk being charged with breaking and entering into our home just to mess around with my computer? Of course, they might have tampered with other things, but why was our house of any interest to them at all?

I put a password on my computer, but that didn't seem to stop it. After I did that, I found my computer tower moved from the indented area where it had been on the carpet, and no one else had been in the house. Again, I have no idea what anyone was after. By this time, I knew something was going on, but I still didn't know what or why. The same key unlocked all our doors, so it seemed likely that whoever was behind this now had the key. Around this time, I realized I was often being followed. At that time, people didn't even try to conceal it. Sometimes one would nudge the other and nod in my direction, as if to say, "There she is." People who were obvious about this when it first started happening seemed to know when I had appointments, and where. The question continued to be this: Why was I being singled out to be followed and spied on?

Being followed is a difficult thing to talk about because many people who think others are "following" them are either paranoid or delusional. I know that I am neither of those. I believe the people behind all this know that as long as they do nothing to get caught, my story will sound delusional, and no one will believe me. I would later learn that this is exactly what organized stalkers think! Having something like this happen to me was so puzzling that it seemed like months went by before I could even believe it. As I look back, I wonder why we didn't change the locks on our doors right away. I think there was a lengthy period of disbelief because there was no explanation for what was happening.

I also noticed an increase in cars driving around our block and around our neighborhood. I had a good view from a second floor window, and I very frequently saw vehicles driving around the block for no apparent reason. Our neighborhood was tucked away, not in a location that would warrant such traffic. The cars would drive in, drive around the block and then leave. Since such strange things had begun to happen, I suspected the increased traffic had something to do with the stalking, but I didn't know what it was. Quite honestly, like most of the things the stalkers do, it just seemed rather ridiculous to me.

Our kitchen table at the time was heavy and had a glass top. It had a light fixture hanging above it. We had that table for several years, and I know that it did not move easily. It stayed in place very well, and it was so heavy that the four feet on the pedestal base holding it made small indentations in the vinyl flooring. One day, after having been gone for a few hours, I came home and found this heavy table moved out of place by several inches! I could tell it was moved from the indentations on the floor, and it was also no longer centered under the light fixture. Of course I tried to find an explanation, but I couldn't. When I later asked Mark if he knew how it had been moved, he said no. Again, nothing else was disturbed in the house, and I had no proof that anything had happened. All I could figure was that someone moved the table to get to the light fixture. But why? What were they doing, and why were they doing it to me, or to us? Over the next few years, I found that table moved several times with no explanation. I was beginning to think that a listening device or camera was in the light. Why else would they move the table?

That was not the only light fixture we had problems with. One day, I noticed that our dining room chandelier was badly broken, and there was a scratch on the dining room table that had never been there before. Again, there was no explanation. The way it was broken could not have happened from cleaning it. It really looked like it had fallen on the table, but it was hanging from the ceiling now. What could I do? I ended up having the fixture replaced. Then, the ceiling light at the back entry door broke. None of us had touched it, but one of the glass panels now had a crack in it. More strange things continued to happen, and I still had no explanation for any of it. Now, as I look back at these things, I realize that this may have been their way of making sure we knew they were coming into our house. However, we were so perplexed by it all that we had no idea what to think.

Also during this time, I noticed that several of our light switch cover plates and electric outlet cover plates looked like they had been loosened. It was fairly obvious that someone had loosened or removed and then replaced the covers for some reason. At that point, we had lived in that house for three years, and I had never noticed anything like that before. A few of our smoke detectors also looked like they had been tampered with.

For years, we almost always went out to dinner as a family on Friday nights. We ate at many different places. One Friday evening, we were leaving the house when I noticed a Jeep driving very slowly around the block. We started talking about where we wanted to eat after we started to drive, and we decided on a certain restaurant that was at least a 20 minute drive away.

There are literally hundreds of restaurants in City A, and dozens of them are in the same area as this restaurant, yet this Jeep drove all the way from our neighborhood to the very same restaurant! Their Jeep was in front of us for most of the way, so I think they had to have heard us talking in our car. I have more evidence of this later. They took a table not too far from us and seemed to watch us the whole time. If that were the only thing that ever happened, I would say it was a coincidence, but this started happening all the time.

In the spring of 1994, we had Cindy evaluated for attention deficit disorder by an educational psychologist in City A. Her teacher had recommended it based on her observations and evaluations of Cindy in the classroom. After the psychologist met with Cindy a few times, she had a conference with Mark and me to discuss her recommendations. She recommended that we start Cindy on a stimulant medication to see if it improved her attention and focus in the classroom. It was a difficult decision for us, and the only reason I am disclosing something so personal is because of a strange remark the psychologist made to us.

She suggested that we tell Cindy's teachers that we were starting the medication. She then seemed slightly irritated and said that she didn't care how they did it in "State N;" in our area of the country, "we like to tell the teachers." We were puzzled by this cryptic remark, and Mark spoke right up and asked her what she meant. She said that there was a doctor who had practiced in State N who advocated not telling the teachers when a child was taking medication for attention deficit disorder. He claimed that waiting to see if the teacher saw a difference in the child was a better indicator that the medication was working than if you told them ahead of time. Anthony Hanson had practiced pediatric medicine in State N for several years before moving to the City A area. That fact did not sink in until later. Was this yet another coincidence, or was he getting involved in our lives? Why?

This was not the first time that something like this happened. Over the years, when talking with various people, I have sensed on numerous occasions that they knew more about me than I had yet told them. In the case of the above remark by the psychologist, I wish that we had followed up with a question about whether this doctor from State N was just someone she had read about or whether he had actually talked to her about Cindy. The only reason she even told us what she did was because Mark and I had looked at each other with puzzled expressions and Mark asked her what she meant.

In July, 1994, Mark, Cindy and I drove to Washington, D.C. I remember we left City A on a Saturday. After driving for about three hours, I noticed a car that was staying near us for quite a few miles, either passing ahead of us or right behind us. I didn't pay too much attention until Mark started to pass it, and for some reason, he asked me to turn around and see what kind of car it was. Maybe Mark had noticed that the car had stayed close to us for quite a few miles. When I looked over as we were passing it, I couldn't believe it. There was Anthony Hanson in the front passenger seat. He kept looking straight ahead until we were past. Another man was driving. Soon after that, their car headed in a different direction, as far as I could tell. Another coincidence? Their car might have been following us all the way from City A.

Our next-door neighbor was a single man in his forties named Daniel Lloyd. He lived on the corner, and the pod of mailboxes for our cul-de-sac was on the street adjacent to the side of his house, across from his driveway. One day, I left to pick up Cindy from school. I sometimes turned right out of our street and drove around the block so I could pull up next to the mailboxes and reach our mail from the left front window of my van. I can only assume that it looked like I had already left the area, because after I drove around the block and approached the mailboxes across from Daniel's house, there was Anthony Hanson standing in Daniel's driveway! It looked like they were about to leave in Daniel's car. He seemed startled to see my van, and he turned around quickly to walk back into the garage. I have no idea what his connection to Daniel Lloyd was or why he was there. I remember it was a Friday afternoon.

I have often found that looking back on certain events or circumstances gives me more insight than when I was actually going through them. It wasn't until after we had moved to City B that I thought about our relationship with Daniel Lloyd. He kept mostly to himself, and we rarely saw him. This was especially true after the day I saw Anthony Hanson at his house. It was too large of a city for that to be a coincidence. I often wonder if Daniel was the neighbor who kept tabs on us at that house. If so, when and how did he get involved? Was Anthony Hanson there that day to check out the monitoring equipment at Daniel's house, or was that the day he first approached Daniel about helping to spy on us? Another option is that they already knew each other, but I believe that is highly unlikely.

My phones and answering machine continued to be tampered with. Also, in 1994 especially, I would get dozens of calls where the person would stay on the line but say nothing and then hang up. My answering machine at that time had a two digit code to call remotely for the messages. The code could not be changed, and it was printed on the machine. Someone was using the code because all of our messages started to disappear, get cut off, etc. I finally bought a new machine with no remote access.

At this point, in 1994, I was talkative about all of this to Mark but to no one else. Who would believe it? Mark said I should forget about it. He had basically decided that since he couldn't figure out why anyone would do this to us and there was no real proof, he didn't want to have to think about it. I did try to forget about it, but things kept happening.

Over the next few years, there was continual evidence that people were entering our house when we were not home. Also, it seemed like anyplace I went, when I returned to my car, there would be someone sitting in a car nearby, almost watching me. They would immediately get on a cell phone, and they would often start their car right after I started mine. This happened dozens and dozens of times. I still believed that Anthony Hanson was involved in some way. In 1996, with some research, I found out that he had moved and was practicing medicine in City X. I believe that somehow, he was still involved in this from wherever he was living.

We were going to celebrate Cindy's eighth birthday with some relatives who lived in City A. Several days before her birthday, I took her to a store with a bakery so she could pick out a special cake for her birthday party. She selected a Disney-themed cake from a book, and I ordered a special personalized birthday message for the cake. On the day of the family party, a Saturday, we discussed at home when I would go pick up the cake before we headed to the party. When I drove to the store to pick it up, something unbelievable happened. I drove into the parking lot and started walking to the store entrance. Just then, a man walked toward me and said the electricity in the store had just gone out, and no one could go in or out since the doors were electric. He said everyone who was already in the store was stuck in there. He seemed to be trying to discourage me from waiting, as he said it might be a while before the electricity came back on. I'm not sure how he would have known that since he appeared to be a customer also.

I didn't have a cell phone in those days so I decided to go wait in my car for a while to see if the electricity came back on. I assumed the store personnel had called the electric company, and maybe it wouldn't be that long. After about ten more minutes of waiting in my car, another man drove into the parking lot and parked right next to me. Only in hindsight did I realize that the whole thing had probably been a setup – more street theater by the stalking group. The man got out of his car, and if he had been a normal customer, he would have started walking toward the doors of the store. Instead, he called out to me as I sat in my car and asked me if something was wrong. Looking back, it is quite obvious that he was in on the "joke" too. I was sitting in my car, minding my own business, and for all he knew, I was waiting for someone to come out of the store. I didn't look distressed or upset at all – there was nothing that would explain why he yelled into my car.

I opened my car window and told him about the electricity in the store. He asked me why I didn't just go to another grocery store, and I told him that I had come to pick up a pre-ordered cake from the bakery. He then said to me, "If I were you, I would go to the ABC Store down the street and pick up a cake from their bakery. They have nice cakes there." Since Mark and Cindy were waiting for me at home, that is what I ended up doing. As one would expect, Cindy was disappointed because she had been excited about having the special cake she had selected. We got over it, but I had a nagging feeling about that day for a long time.

It seemed to me that if this had been a real life random occurrence, neither of the men in the parking lot would have said what they did. They both seemed more concerned with getting me to leave the store than with their own reasons for being there. Of course, I will never know what really happened, but I suspect that the two guys were in on it, and maybe one of them was even an electric company employee who knew how to shut the power off to that store. They might have been hurrying me along so they could restore the power. It is a rather big deal to shut off the power to a grocery store!

The next day, I called the bakery manager and told her that I had tried to pick up the cake the day before, but their electricity was off and I couldn't get into the store. I explained that I waited for a while, but we were expected for a birthday party so I had to quickly make other arrangements for a cake. She was not very happy about the cake because it was personalized, and she then told me that the electricity hadn't been off for very long. Apparently, it was only off during the exact period of time I was in the parking lot! How odd. I told her that I had no way of knowing when it would come back on. If this was indeed another prank of the stalkers, just what was their game plan that day? To prevent me from picking up my daughter's birthday cake? How pathetic. The real person who was hurt in this case was an eight-year-old girl. I have to think that most mature people would think it was idiotic that grown men would participate in a game of keeping me away from a cake!

In early 1996, I did some grant writing for an organization in State A. The first time I met with the director, she gave me a stack of materials she thought would be helpful. It was mostly information on their organization and other things she pulled from her files. I looked through everything, and I kept the materials for a few months. I kept them in a separate stack so I wouldn't misplace anything of hers. When I returned them, she took a minute to look through them and to recall what she had given me. She paused for a second and looked puzzled, and she showed me a brochure on the XYZ Foundation from a year or two before. I asked if she had given that to me with everything else, and she said she hadn't. I knew it wasn't mine, so she said she would just keep it. The XYZ Foundation is associated with the university where Anthony Hanson went to medical school. I know I did not put the brochure there.

During 1994-95, my one-year-old van with very low mileage started to have flat tires. I had probably only had one flat tire in my life, and then my van had four flat tires (actually five) in less than one year! Each time, they found a nail or a screw in the tire, so I just had to chalk it up to coincidence. We were not around any more construction than usual, so what could I think? It seemed that every tire on my van systematically got a flat. Each time except one, Mark was with me, and he would put on the spare or get someone to do it. I would then take it to a nearby tire store and get the tire repaired. They were always holes that could be patched. We were never at home when it happened. Usually, we were shopping or at a restaurant, and when we came out, Mark noticed a flat tire.

However, one time that year, I discovered a flat tire while my car was in our garage. I called AAA to come put my spare on. The dispatcher took the information, and she told me the AAA driver knew how to get to my house because he would be the same man who had been to my house a few weeks before when I had the previous flat tire. I told her she must be mistaken because AAA had never been to my house before, but it didn't really matter as long as he got there. I didn't say a word about it to the driver, but he also brought it up! He said that he was at my house and had put on the spare tire on the same van a few weeks before. He seemed very sure of himself, but I told him that he was mistaken. I asked if it might have been another house in the same neighborhood, but he said no. He said a tall woman in a robe was there when he put the spare tire on the last time.

This would later turn out to be an important point. He seemed very sure of himself, and he was not going to budge on his story, but since it didn't matter at that moment, I let it go. Looking back, I probably should have asked for their records for the alleged service call, but instead, I just assumed they were wrong. If this stranger was actually at our house, she must have had an identical van. I wish I had followed up on it and asked if they had noted the license plate. As the years went by, I began to suspect that when they entered our house, they most likely drove a vehicle identical to one of ours – probably mine – and drove right into the garage.

Since all my tires now had patches on them, I started to feel a little unsafe. We finally decided to buy a whole new set of tires for the van. The very day I had the new tires put on, I went to the grocery store. When I came out of the store, one of my brand-new tires already had a flat tire – another nail! I couldn't believe it, and neither could the tire store. Now I already had a patch in one of my brand-new tires. This was way too much to be a coincidence.

I knew that someone was coming into our home while we were not there. I would find things slightly different, but at that point, I never found anything missing. I did find things scratched, tampered with, or slightly moved out of place. A few times, I found that my clothes had been tampered with or damaged. I had purchased a beaded sequined top, which I planned to wear to an upcoming event. It had never been worn, and I would never have bought it if it had smelled. One day, I went to look at it and hold it up to the skirt I planned to wear it with. I was very surprised to find that it now stunk with a very strong odor. Another time, I found one of my long robes with the bottom hem completely torn out. There was no way it was like that the last time I had worn it.

Apparently, it is not that hard to compromise someone else's electronic garage door, especially if you have the code for their opener. I also knew that one time, I had heard someone in our house while I was there. What I still didn't know was why anyone would go to all this trouble and risk just to spy on or victimize us.

Around November, 1995, I was so frustrated I decided to try something. Since we had two phone lines at home and I felt they were probably both bugged, I called one number from the other. I said the call was for Anthony Hanson and that I had received an anonymous letter telling me everything about what had been going on. I said that the letter gave all kinds of details about how my house and phones were bugged, etc., and how he was behind all of it. I said I wanted to know why he was doing all of this to me and my family.

Soon after the phone call, I came home one day and found the carpeting pulled up from the wall in several places. As I looked more closely, I also found that the plastic mirror brackets on the bathroom plate glass mirrors had been loosened. It looked as if someone was looking for something that was hidden. If I were going to hide a piece of paper, I would never have even thought about putting it under the carpet or behind a plate glass mirror, but apparently someone was looking for something or wanted me to think that. What scared me the most about this was wondering who I might be dealing with. I knew the condition and placement of everything in my house, and I knew the carpet was not loose in several places, and the mirror brackets had never been loose. Once again, however, what point could I make?

All kinds of strange things continued to happen on our phones. I have no idea what they might have done to our phones, but when the phone company finally found an illegal interception on one of our lines (in State B), I was not at all surprised. One evening, I hit the redial button on my phone and it connected me to a medical answering service. I know that was not the last number I had called. In fact, I had never even heard of them. That was right after my phone rang, and the caller had hung up after I answered. I began to wonder if there was a way my calls were being forwarded to another number. Another time, I picked up the phone to make a call. There was no dial tone, but there were people talking in the background. It sounded like their phone was off the hook. I listened for a few minutes, and finally a man yelled, "I found the tape!" Someone finally hung up the phone. That was not the last time that would happen.

Soon after that, I called the phone company and made a general complaint about our phone service. I believe I said something about the fact that it seemed like maybe "our line was crossed with someone else's." That was the only way I could think of to explain it. The phone company rep said they would have someone check the line. A few days later, I answered the phone one evening. A man on the other end asked for someone by name, and I said he must have the wrong number. He then started to laugh, and there was a lot of noise in the background. He said that maybe we had our "lines crossed." Of course, no one could possibly have known about that conversation unless our phone had been tapped. Over and over, the types of things the organized stalkers do reveal what sick and sordid individuals they are. He sounded like a grown man, but it seemed like a junior high school prank.

During the time we lived in City A, I did some of our banking using the automated phone system of our bank. They didn't yet have online banking at that time. The main reason I would do this was to transfer funds from our savings account to our checking account. Each time, I would have to enter account numbers and my pass code for phone access to our bank accounts. Each time I called, the system would also give me the option of hearing account balances for any accounts we had with the bank. I started to worry that if our phones were tapped, the people involved could tamper with our bank accounts in some way or have access to our account balance information. I never found any problems on the bank statements, but I still wondered about it.

I decided to go into the local branch to find out what I would need to do to see a listing of phone access history to our accounts. I talked to the branch manager, and of course she told me to change my pass code right away and to watch for any discrepancies in my bank statement. I confided in her that I believed someone was illegally tapping our phone line, and a new pass code would soon become known to them. My only option would be to change the pass code from a different phone and never use our home phone for banking again.

The branch manager said she would check into it and get back to me. A few days later, someone else from the main bank office called me and said that they would not be able to recreate a history of phone attempts to access our accounts. I had sort of figured that would be the way it turned out. However, several days later, I received a letter from the local branch of our bank. The branch manager had simply photocopied the response to her original request for the information. They had looked into it after all. It showed that in the previous month, there had been over two hundred phone inquiries into our bank account balances! This was something no one could do without our account numbers AND pass code. It said that they did not have a listing of which phone numbers called in, just the number of inquiries.

When I said I used the automated phone system on occasion, I was talking about one or two times a month – not over two hundred times! Neither Mark nor I ever even used it to check account balances, just to transfer funds occasionally. Now I was sure that not only was someone checking our balances, but more than one person was doing so. Even if one person was checking our accounts every day, that would still only be 30 inquiries a month at the most. This new information was so obscure that I had no idea what it might prove or what to do with it. The bank said that everyone called the same number for automated banking, and they would have no way of tracing which phone numbers were accessing our specific accounts.

Starting in 1996, in City A, I began to notice a rather tall woman who seemed to show up at the same places and at the same times that I did. For instance, I saw her in the mall before Cindy's dance lesson, at Target, and walking along the street where I was driving on a few occasions. It seemed odd that I would see the same woman so often, but she never spoke to me or acknowledged me. I'm almost certain that she was the same woman I have seen several times since, in City B and City C. She was about the same height and frame as the woman I had seen in City A. She looked different each time, but I can't help but wonder how she is involved in this. I thought back to what the AAA driver had said about the tall woman at my house. None of it made sense.

Also, during the years in City A, I had a very definite feeling that there had been two men in our bedroom in the middle of the night on several occasions. This went on for several years, even in the next two houses we lived in, and it didn't stop until measures were taken to physically make it too difficult to enter the house while we were home. Even then, it still happened sometimes. The feelings I had were always the same – it was as if I wanted to wake up, but I just couldn't quite wake up enough to realize what was going on. If I wake up under normal circumstances, I certainly know what it feels like. For instance, if I wake up at 2:00 a.m. and realize that Mark fell asleep on the sofa while watching television, I might feel sleepy, but I would get out of bed to wake him up and tell him to come to bed. If Cindy came into our bedroom during a thunderstorm, I would fully remember that happening. However, each time, I would slightly wake up and realize that there were two men in our bedroom. I can only say that I felt like what I think I would feel like if I were drugged in some way.

It is such a dark and scary thought that I don't think I could even grasp the possibility for a long time. Even after I was positive that we had intruders in our home while we were away and that I was being stalked for some reason, it took a long time to believe that people were entering when we were asleep. It is even harder to imagine what they were doing. That alone is enough to give me nightmares to this day. If they drugged me in some way, I know they must have drugged Mark also. What about Cindy?

As I have thought about it over time, I have sometimes wondered if the two men in the room could have anything to do with the two women I have seen together on numerous occasions. I have sometimes wondered if there is a possibility that they are the same people.

In March, 1997, Mark accepted a position with a company in City B, over a thousand miles away. We assumed that moving so far away would put an end to all of this, but it didn't. Little did we know what control they felt they needed over us. Even the sale of our house in City A had some strange aspects to it. Mark started his new job in City B within a few weeks, and I stayed in City A to handle the sale of our house and get ready for the move. We listed the house, and a day or two later, the real estate agent called and told me there was a showing scheduled. Cindy and I left the house and came back after they were gone. I figured that we should get used to this routine, as I knew that it might take a while to sell the house. About a day later, our agent called and said the people who saw the house were making a full price offer on it! What great news!

We accepted their offer, and a day or two later, the real estate agent said the buyers wanted to come see the house again "to check out a few things." I said it would be fine, but since they wanted to come over at night, I asked if I could stay home. I assured her that I would stay out of the way. The man showed up with his real estate agent, and she and I talked while he went to check things out. Of all the strange things, all he seemed to want to check out was the attic! We had lived in that house for almost six years, and I don't believe we had ever been in the attic. However, since the stalking and home intrusions started, I had found little pieces of attic insulation in my closet on occasion. (The only attic access was in the master bedroom closet.) Since that was new to me, I had no way to explain it. The buyer gave an explanation of wanting to see the attic in case he decided to so some remodeling at a later time. He must have spent at least 30 minutes up there. When he came down through the closet ceiling opening, a few more pieces of insulation fell down, and it reminded me of those stray pieces I had seen on occasion. He also went down to the basement for a few minutes, and then they left.

Looking back, I suspect that the quick sale, at such a good price, might have had something to do with what was in the attic. Several years ago, I called a neighbor from our street in City A, and she said the couple who bought our house had divorced and moved away about two years after they moved in.

CHAPTER TWO

1997 – 1999: CITY B

After Mark closed on our new house in City B (this was in 1997), he flew back to City A to be there for the move and to drive Cindy and me to City B. He had been given several duplicate house keys, and he left all the extras on the kitchen counter in our new house. I later found out that while we were driving to City B, the sidelight window by our front door had been broken, and the builder hurried to replace it before we got there. At that time, the builder's superintendent still had access to our house to finish a few things. I know this could happen to anyone, but it was a bad way to start off. At that point in time, we thought the stalking was over, and we didn't even have the locks changed. In our next two houses, one of the first things I did was to have the locks changed and to add additional deadbolts.

The new house was pre-wired with a security system, but when they came to activate it, they had a difficult time. The installer said he had never had so many problems, and he asked me if anyone had messed with it. It took them a long time (a few days) to figure it out and get it to work correctly. Looking back, I'm sure the stalkers had probably tampered with it in an effort to make the system capable of being bypassed. They are probably the ones who broke the front sidelight window, and all they had to do was make a copy of one of the keys that were out on the kitchen counter.

I know for a fact that people were in that house while we were gone, while we were sleeping, and while the security system was armed. I don't know how they did it, but they did. Not too many months after we moved in, I started to notice strange things about some of the light fixtures there. For one thing, one day I noticed that the bottom link on both of our chandeliers was all scratched up. I know they had not been like that before because I would have noticed it. I called the electrician to see if he could replace the scratched links, and he asked if someone had taken the fixtures down because the links that were scratched would probably be the links that would have to be bent to remove the fixtures. The chain links do not scratch like that by themselves, or even by cleaning them. The only way they could get that scratched was by someone twisting them to remove or replace the fixture. I knew that no one had taken the fixtures down with my knowledge.

As time went on, I noticed that the brass links on both the kitchen and dining room light fixtures were slowly being replaced, from the bottom up, with a slightly different shaped brass link. The ones at the top were more oval, and the new ones being replaced were more rounded. It was as if each time the light fixture was taken down, someone had to replace the scratched bottom link with a new one, and they couldn't find an identical link to the ones already there. Since I had talked to the electrician about the problem, the intruders must have realized they couldn't keep scratching the links. It seemed obvious to me that for some reason, someone was continuing to take down these fixtures to do something.

The bathroom light fixtures were also tampered with. There is no one in my family who would have touched them. These light fixture strips were above the large plate glass mirrors over the sinks. One had to stand on a ladder or on the vanity to reach them. When we first moved in, I stood on the vanities and dusted the fixtures and bulbs. One day, I noticed that one of the fixtures in the master bathroom looked loose. I checked it out and found that it had been loosened. Several of the cups around the bulbs were loose, as if someone had taken the whole light strip down. I looked at the other bathrooms, and I found the same thing with the light fixture above Cindy's sink. No one had done any work on them, and they had never been touched, except to dust them. This couldn't have happened by simply dusting them. Someone had taken them down for some reason.

We received a phone bill a few months after we moved in with all sorts of erroneous charges on it for a pager service, 800 service, and voicemail, etc. There were several companies involved, and it took me months to get it all straightened out. By then, someone had a few free months of all those services. How did this happen? First of all, the companies involved said the calls had come from our home number without a doubt. They played the tape recording of the order, which was electronic. The voice was not one of us, and it was a whisper. They finally agreed to drop all the erroneous charges, and I was supposed to just forget it happened.

As part of their internal controls, they were sup-posed to call the number back and confirm that the order was placed legitimately. However, this particular number was answered by our fax machine, and so they would never be able to check. We could call out from that number, but incoming calls were answered by the fax machine. When I informed the phone company about this, they said they would send someone out to check the line. I was then informed that they had found an illegal interception on the phone line! That meant that our phone line was being used in two locations! That was their explanation as to how the erroneous charges were made to our line. When I asked for more information about who was using our line, I was told we would need a court order to find out any more.

When we first moved into our house in City B, I was swamped by telemarketers selling everything. I know they are notified of new homeowners and that this was to be expected. I had never done anything to block their calls. However, after we lived there for a few months, all calls from telemarketers stopped. Completely. When I was at a neighborhood gathering, several neighbors complained about how many calls they received. I'm all for submitting my phone number to the "Do Not Call" registry, but at that time, I didn't know about it. Did someone else submit our number to block all telemarketers, or were our calls going somewhere else first? Every once in a while, I would get the usual couple of telemarketer calls a day for a few days, and then they stopped again. One theory I had was that if someone was going to all the trouble to record our calls, he or she wouldn't want to mess with telemarketer calls and therefore submitted our number to the "Do Not Call" registry.

Cindy went on an overnight class trip with the fifth graders in May, 1998. They were gone on Wednesday and Thursday night. A slight emergency came up with Cindy on Wednesday afternoon, and one of the teachers called the school principal back in City B to see if she wanted to notify us. She called me on Thursday morning and said she had tried to reach us Wednesday night, but she had to leave a message on our answering machine. I told her that I never got a message and that we had been home all evening, and I asked if she could have dialed the wrong number. She repeated the number, the one she had just called again that morning. It was our home number. Yet, she said that when she dialed it the night before, an electronic voice answered, repeated our number, and said to leave a message. It certainly seemed like someone was forwarding our calls or using our number in a second location.

Another example similar to this had to do with a repair I needed done to our front door. The builder told me that XXX Building Supply would be calling me to set up a time to come out. A few weeks went by, and there was no call. I talked to the builder's superintendent, and he said he assumed it had been taken care of and that he would look into it. When he called me back, he said that XXX Building Supply claimed they had called me twice, and I said it was okay to come out both times. When they got there, no one was home. I told the superintendent that was not true; I had not received a single call from them. I was never able to talk to the person who actually said it, but it made me uncomfortable. Again, if that were the only strange thing to ever happen to me, I might assume that XXX Building Supply was trying to cover up the fact that they had never really called me, but the superintendent said he was positive about it. Were these more calls that went to someone else and not to our home phone?

As I have continued to say, I knew our house pretty well, and I knew when something was moved or scratched, etc. One more example of this was with a folding table I had recently bought and had delivered from an office supply store. We bought it as a work table for Cindy to use for doing homework. Mark and I moved it into an upstairs bedroom. Cindy was out of town visiting Mark's parents at the time. Then Mark and I went out of town for a few days. When we returned, I again had the feeling that someone had been in our house. The next day, I looked at the brand-new table, and it had a big deep gouge in it. It had to have been something sharp to have gone through the laminated top, and I know the scratch was not there before we left. None of us had even put anything on the table. This incident had to have been malicious, and it made me begin to wonder how many of the damages to our belongings were the same.

When we lived in City B, Mark had to travel to Los Angeles for business quite often for about a year. It was during those times that I remember the same feeling of two men in my bedroom in the middle of the night. The master bedroom was on the first floor, and Cindy's bedroom was on the second floor. Sometimes when Mark was out of town, Cindy would sleep in my bed. She had a few favorite stuffed animals she liked to sleep with, and she would put them in the bed next to her. One night, I woke up when I felt something hit me. Just as I woke up, very groggy, two men were standing by Cindy's side of the bed, and one of them said something about how I could sleep with the animal that had just been thrown at me (a beanie baby toy). I felt so sleepy. I saw that Cindy was sound asleep, and I simply could not keep my eyes open as I saw these men leave the room. The next day, I remembered the stuffed animal event with some clarity, but Cindy had no memory of it. She had slept (or was drugged) through the whole thing.

Another strange thing that happened several times had to do with my car radio, in both my current car at that time and my previous car. Mark and Cindy and I had all been in the car when it had happened, and there was no explanation. We almost always have the car radio on. On several occasions, it went completely silent for several seconds, with absolutely no noise coming from it. If we changed stations or touched the volume, it was still totally silent. Then it would come back on. It was very strange that it happened several times in two different vehicles. Since I believe our vehicles have had listening devices in them, it made me wonder how that might be connected to it.

There is something in the dark world of organized group stalking that is referred to as street theater. It involves a planned performance by one or more people who make sure they are in the location that the target or victim will be. These sorts of things have happened to me on numerous occasions. They somehow contact each other to give the organized stalking members a chance to be there for the entertainment. I am amazed by how dumb some of these plots are, but nevertheless, they go on frequently.

One weekend, I noticed an ad in the newspaper for a shoe sale at a mall department store. The sale was for a specific brand and style of shoe that I liked. I have a narrow foot, and sometimes I have trouble finding shoes. I called the store to make sure they had my size in stock. The salesperson said that they had just received a large shipment, and they had plenty of stock in my size. Later that day, I headed for the store.

When I got to the shoe area, I asked a salesperson for that specific shoe in my size. A few minutes later, a different salesperson came over to where I was sitting. He said that he was sorry, but a woman had just come into the store and purchased every single pair of that shoe in my size. He said he had never seen anything like it. He said there were several pairs, and the customer had even bought two of the same color. She told him she wanted every single pair of shoes in that style and size. He said she had to make two trips to carry them all to her car! The shoe area was rather crowded that day, so although I was out of luck as far as buying that shoe, apparently the stalker crowd thought it would be entertaining to watch. How pathetic.

Mark and Cindy and I went on an out-of-town trip over the Fourth of July weekend in 1997. By then, I was used to having things happen even when we were out of town. It seemed that the people involved in this could track us down anywhere, and did! One afternoon, we went to an outlet mall in the area because I wanted to go to a certain store. As I was looking around, I saw a man walking around, alone, and he seemed like he was interested in what we were looking at. He didn't seem otherwise interested in the merchandise in the store. I had become very perceptive over the past few years. Well, we did buy a few things, and Mark took them to the car because we were going to look at some other stores.

About a half hour later, we headed across the parking lot, and I saw the man I had noticed earlier in the factory store with a group of people heading toward the parking lot. I couldn't believe it. In the group of three women and three men was a man I had seen ever so often since the stalking had begun in City A! He was looking at a brochure and didn't look up at us at all! We were just yards away from them. Was this just another coincidence? Why was the other man in their group in the store watching us earlier?

Another strange thing happened one evening when Mark and I flew back from L.A. to City B. When we got off the plane, there was a man standing there, by himself, watching everyone get off the plane. He was standing back from everyone else, so I noticed him. Once Mark and I headed for the luggage pick-up area, he started walking behind us. We picked up our luggage and headed for the parking lot. As we approached our car, I saw the same man standing outside his car. He was parked right in front of us! As soon as we got there, he nodded at us and got in his car and left. He didn't have any luggage and he wasn't with anyone. It seemed like he was spying on us, and he wasn't even being discreet about it. He wanted us to know that he was watching us. It seems that most of the time when these things happened, we had talked about where we were going while we were in the car or in our house, or we made the reservation or appointment by phone.

I talked earlier about the car radio going completely silent on occasion and how this happened five or six times in two different cars. A few months after we moved into our house in City B, a single man, John Vinson, bought a vacant new house across the street. He said he had relocated from another city and was employed by X Corporation. The city he had moved from was quite close to City A, where we had just relocated from.

One evening, I left to go to the grocery store, and he pulled out right behind me. He ended up following me to the grocery store, and on the way there, the same strange thing happened with the car radio! It went completely silent for almost a minute. I thought this was odd, but I didn't know what to think about it. Although Mark had met him already, I hadn't. Since I knew he had driven to the same store, I decided to introduce myself in the parking lot. He said hello, but there was little conversation. He seemed surprised that I even knew he was there.

After several months, I still had a funny feeling about him. I am not saying that his transfer to City B had anything to do with us living there, but something seemed strange about him. Maybe he was one of the game players in this crazy spy game. I knew that he had started to use the same house cleaning service that I used every few weeks, although they cleaned his house on a different day. One evening, I started talking out loud, inside my house, as if I were on the phone. Mark wasn't home, and Cindy was upstairs. I went on about how the cleaning service people had told me they had found something about me in his house, and how I knew he was spying on us. I talked for about five minutes, and I knew he was home at the time. After all, if I was wrong about everything that was going on, what harm would it do? If there were no transmitters in our house, no one would even hear me, as should be the case in an ideal world!

However, within a day or two, he and his dog were gone for good! He left all of his belongings, but he never returned until after we moved to the City C area. The house cleaning service was never at his house again, but he still owned the house. He just didn't live there. He did have a lawn care company take care of his lawn. The only time we saw him (accidentally) was one Sunday when we were leaving to go on a trip. We got about ten minutes from home when we decided to return home to get something we forgot. That was when we saw him drive into his driveway for the first time in months! Another coincidence? Apparently, he showed up a few other times when we were not there, but we never saw him there again. He moved back in after we moved to City C.

In retrospect, the similarities between John Vinson and Daniel Lloyd (our next door neighbor in City A) are definitely there. They were both single men in their forties, living alone. They both had dogs. They both moved into suburban neighborhoods with single family homes mostly populated by married couples with children. They both lived within yards of our house. I feel fairly certain that they were both involved in spying on us. If there was at least one nearby stalker-occupied house in the first two places we lived since this began, I have to believe in hindsight that there have been others in the next houses we lived in.

I had still not talked to anyone except Mark about all the strange things that were going on because it was so obviously bizarre. Looking back, it might have been beneficial to find out where John Vinson lived from 1998 to 1999, and why he moved out of his house for that extended period of time. I don't think the other neighbors knew him very well when he left, and I never asked them if they knew where he went. We did find out that he moved back in after we moved away.

Something else that started happening while we lived in this house was the huge increase in small planes that flew over our house. We went from hardly ever noticing any to frequently having planes fly right over or circle over our house. A few times, I noticed a plane flying over when I left to go pick up Cindy from school. As I was waiting outside, the same plane continued circling the school. Since there was no way to know what they were doing, I didn't get too concerned. This ended up being something that would go on for years, both in City B and City C. It was also something that I would later find out was fairly common in organized stalking. In City C, we also frequently have helicopters fly directly over our house.

In June, 1999, we went to Arizona and Nevada on vacation. We were at a quaint shopping area in Sedona, Arizona when a man, a woman, and a small child followed us into a shop. I remember that he had a T-shirt from a university that was about an hour away from where we lived in City A. They stayed in the background for a while, and then we kept shopping. That evening, we left Sedona for Flagstaff, where we stopped for dinner at one of the many restaurants there. About halfway through dinner, the same man seemed to go out of his way to walk by our table. Of all the places in Arizona, they picked the same shop at the same shopping center in Sedona and the same restaurant at the same time in Flagstaff! Coincidence? They arrived at the restaurant after us because Mark said he saw them come in.

Since 1994, it has seemed that even when we have rented a car while on vacation, stalkers have always found us easily. I have no doubt that they hid a GPS on every car we owned and every rental car we rented. I feel that I need to say once again that we are ordinary people – not celebrities. I have no idea how we were selected for this game, but we were. I have to believe that the Internet is heavily used in these activities. Just for the sake of example, suppose there are several thousand people in the U.S. who are familiar with this alleged "stalker network" website. As soon as someone knew our travel plans for the trip to Arizona and Nevada, he could post our plans on the website. Then, if someone lived in Sedona or was planning to be in Sedona on the same days we were, they would take it from there. There was more street theater following us and generally letting us know that we were under surveillance.

We drove from Arizona to Las Vegas, and we were going to fly back to City B from there. On the same flight to City B was the same tall woman I had seen several times before. She was seated next to a young woman in her late teens or early twenties, and they seemed to know each other. Also, although she was not seated with her, another woman I had seen before was also on the plane. I don't know how to explain it, but I believe the second woman was a male cross dresser or transgender individual. It is possible that they both were. I had seen these same two women together a few times before. We went to Chicago for a few days after Thanksgiving in 1996, and I saw them both in the restroom at Marshall Field's in Chicago! They were both there, but again, they acted like they were not together. One of them was dressed as if she were a runway model, including makeup. Although she was an attractive woman, I believe she was actually a man. The other one was dressed casually and was putting on some makeup she had apparently just bought. I noticed because it was the same brand of makeup I had worn for years. Maybe they are both men dressed as women, and maybe they are even the same two men who have been in our house on numerous occasions. They always showed up at the same places we planned to go. They also never seemed to acknowledge me or make eye contact.

Also, on the above mentioned flight from Las Vegas to City B, I believe there were some law enforcement people of some kind. I don't know how to explain it, but it appeared that way to me. There were at least four of them, and one was sitting in the aisle seat one row behind me, next to one of the woman I recognized. They never said a word to each other, at least that I saw. Also, the men and at least one woman who I thought were in law enforcement of some sort never spoke to each other. They all seemed to have serious expressions on their faces and didn't really speak to anyone else.

However, in light of the fact that one of these people was sitting right next to one of the people I believe was involved in the stalking activities, it is entirely possible that these "law enforcement" types were also part of the stalking group. Maybe they were all together on the flight. After all these years, I still don't know what is going on or the full array of people who are involved.

When we returned from our trip, I noticed that 61 caller ID entries were deleted from the phone in the master bedroom. The phone always showed the last 99 entries unless the electricity went out. There were now only 38 entries. If the caller ID was disturbed by a power outage, other clocks in the same room always went out, too. One of these had no battery backup, yet it was not flashing. I believe that someone reset the clock but was not able to do anything about the lost caller ID numbers. They may not have even realized that the caller ID entries were disturbed by a power outage. I think that turning off the power to our house might have had something to do with being able to bypass the security system, at least in City B. That situation presented itself several times in that house.

As I said, we moved into a new house in City B. I pretty much went over everything in the house to note any problems. One day, I saw that the plastic covering over the cold water faucet handle in the laundry room sink was cracked. It had not been cracked before or I would have noticed it. I called the plumber to see where I could get a replacement. He said that a plumber would drop off a new plastic clip covering the next time he was in the neighborhood. These are small, inexpensive items, but I didn't know where I could find one that was exactly the same size. When the plumber came by, he gave me two of them. Since I had an extra one, I put it in a drawer. When I pried out the cracked one, it looked much older than the one on the other faucet handle, and the entire bottom was dirty and deteriorated and cracked. I took off the good one on the other faucet handle to compare it, and it looked just like you would expect a new one to look. Again, I couldn't explain it, but I forgot about it. A few weeks later, the other one was cracked! This time, I knew I had a spare one, so I took the newly cracked one off. It was not the same plastic clip I had just looked at a few weeks before! Again, this one now looked old and deteriorated. I am completely sure it was not the same clip. Those handles did not leak at all, and there is no way that this piece of plastic could crack and deteriorate in two weeks. Without a doubt, someone, for some reason, replaced our newer plastic faucet clips with older, cracked, deteriorated ones. This was either another sick mind game, like the flat tires, or someone really wanted those newer faucet clips and replaced them with their own older versions.

One day, I was watching the television in the master bedroom while I rode my stationary bike. The channel I was watching was not coming in very well, and I checked the cable connection to the television to see if it was loose. Even though I barely touched it, the entire cable connection went out. I then checked the connection in the wall, which was behind a heavy dresser. It was connected but not screwed in tightly, as if someone had unscrewed it. There was no reason for it to be loose as no one had been in the house who would have loosened it. That is the same portable T.V. set that I had noticed was tampered with before. One day, I noticed that the back and the front parts of the set did not match up like they had previously. It was as if someone had taken the T.V. apart.

Something else that went on for a long time involved a loud noise, like a very loud click, from the inside of the same portable T.V. The only times I heard it were late at night and when the set was off. It was loud enough that it woke me from a sound sleep on several occasions. Several times, I heard it just as I was falling asleep. I probably heard it at least fifty times over the years.

In January, 1999, I came home one afternoon and noticed two things that were different. First, the cords (electric and cable) on the T.V. in the breakfast nook had been messed with. The television was on a baker's rack, and the cords were always tucked behind the rack. Now they were out, which would happen if someone had pulled the rack out or taken the television set off the rack.

The second thing was the brass cover on the bathroom light strip above one of the sinks in the master bath. This brass cover had no defined top or bottom. Both sides were identical, except this light strip was the one that I had the electrician tighten after we moved in. When he was replacing the brass cover, he pointed out a scratched area on one of the long sides. He said that he could probably get us a new one, or he could just put that side on the top and it wouldn't be noticeable. I said to go ahead and put that side on the top. Then, when I looked at it this time, the scratched part was on the bottom side! I got up on the counter to see if it was a different scratch, but it wasn't. It appeared that the top side was now on the bottom. In order to take it off, one had to remove 8 light bulbs! Why did that fixture have to be removed?

Someone who knows about surveillance equipment might say that with all the evidence we had about someone messing with our light fixtures, it would seem obvious that there were electronic devices of some sort hidden in them. I do suspect that they probably used the light fixtures in some capacity. They have been tampered with in every house we have lived in since the stalking started. There is also a possibility that they know we think that, so they continue to mess with them just to make us think that is the case. Or it could be some of both.

The light fixture over our kitchen table had five separate globes and bulbs. One day, one of the bulbs burned out, and I replaced it with a brand-new GE clear bulb. Two weeks later, the very same bulb burned out. When I went to replace it, I knew that the burned-out bulb was not the same one I had put in two weeks ago. It looked like a very old bulb, and it was not a GE bulb.

CHAPTER THREE

CONTACTING THE FBI IN CITY B

In February, 1999, I sent a letter and documentation about what was happening to the FBI in City B. It included the real names of the people I suspected and the events that had occurred up to that date. I really didn't know where else to turn since I had never had much I could tell the local law enforcement about. I knew we were having continual break-ins to our homes and cars, our phones were probably tapped, etc., but I knew of nothing that had been taken although there had been plenty of damage to our homes and belongings.

I checked in with the FBI office on several occasions, always calling from a pay phone or a cell phone. In 1999, my research told me that cell phones were difficult to intercept. Every time I called, they told me that my case had been turned over to a squad, but they couldn't give me any information. This went on for several months. A few times, they mentioned that they didn't usually handle stalking cases but that my file had been assigned for investigation anyway.

In the fall of 1999, Mark accepted a new position in City C. He started his job in September, and Cindy and I moved in October. A few weeks before we were going to move, I contacted the FBI in City B again to check on the status of their investigation. City B is a large city, and I was told that they had recently opened a suburban office closer to where I lived. He said my case had been transferred to that office. Even though we were moving, I made one last call. The agent in charge at the new location said he had reviewed my complaint. Then he said, "We just don't go investigating private citizens." Since I was busy getting ready for our move, I realized I couldn't do much more with them.

It would be 2003 before I tried to seek the help of the FBI again, this time in City C.

CHAPTER FOUR

1999 – 2003: CITY C

I had the same hope of finally getting away from this awful nightmare when Mark's new job took us to the City C area. I don't know why I thought there might be a chance it would end when it had followed us on every trip and on a previous out-of-state move. I really hoped and prayed it would stop with this move. We bought a house that would be ready in about 5 months, and this necessitated moving into an apartment during that time.

Strange things did begin to happen, even in the temporary apartment. One evening in November, 1999, I looked out through the shades of the bedroom windows. There was a woman standing in the parking lot outside our window. She was just standing there, as if she were trying to hear something. When she saw me looking out, she immediately started walking fast and then running across the parking lot. It was dark, but it appeared that she ran toward one of the other buildings in the apartment complex. I believe it looked like the wife of Anthony Hanson. I was able to see an Internet picture of her from information a private investigator gave me (see below).

There was a tall woman with very long, straight hair in one of the buildings this woman was running toward that night. She looked like the same woman I had seen on other occasions in City A and City B. She also looked very much like the woman I would meet at a luncheon a few years later. I only saw her by accident one day when I left the apartment complex and then immediately drove back in through another entrance. She had apparently left her apartment right after I did and got into a car. I later got the license plate number (New Jersey) as well as another New Jersey plate, which belonged to a man who I believe also lived in the same apartment. There may not have been a connection, but I was looking for anything that might help. This apartment complex had a number of furnished apartments for people working in the city short-term or for people who were relocating and might need temporary housing on a month-to-month basis.

I decided to go see a private investigator. The whole story is so hard to believe that I decided to start with a small step. Since I believed that one of the common denominators was Anthony Hanson, I hired the investigator to do a background search on him. There wasn't anything too helpful in his background, but the search showed that his current home and place of work were in City X. It also identified his wife, Rachel Jones Hanson. She was affiliated with a university in State X. When I checked the university's website, it showed her picture. I was surprised when I realized that she appeared to have been the woman who had watched Cindy's dance class in City A, and I could also swear that she was the woman who was standing outside our apartment in City C.

It still seemed that Anthony Hanson, maybe his wife, and two rather tall, thin women were involved in all of this. That would be in addition to all the hundreds (or thousands) of stalker group members who seemed to follow us everywhere and carry out many of the other things they did.

We moved into our house in March, 2000, and one night in April, 2000, I fell out of bed in the middle of the night and broke my toe. One reason this is so very strange is that I have never fallen out of bed in my life, either before that night or after. I have never walked in my sleep, either. That night, for some unknown reason, I apparently crawled to the end of the bed and crawled right off the bed. As I was stepping off the end of the bed, my right foot caught between the footboard and the mattress, and it basically snapped all my toes, breaking one toe and badly bruising the others. I fell hard to the ground, but when I woke up, I again felt as if I had been drugged. I really think that it was only the painful fall that woke me up at all. With as much pain as I was in, I still felt compelled to climb back into bed and go to sleep. I was so very sleepy that I wasn't fully aware of what had happened. Mark never woke up, even when I was crying out in pain. I later realized that he must have been drugged also. The next day, Mark had no recollection of any of it.

As my memory of that night slowly started to come back, sort of in flashbacks, I remember seeing two men in the room after I climbed back into bed. One was in the corner behind a chair, and the other was standing in the doorway. It was dark, and I immediately went back to sleep only to awake in the morning with three very swollen and sore toes. It is not like me to have been so groggy, and after having broken my foot, it seems highly unlikely that I'd simply climb back in bed to go to sleep. As I said, it was also not like me to climb off the end of the bed while I was asleep.

We went to an urgent care center the next day, and X-rays showed that only one toe was broken. My toes were taped, and I wore a special shoe for weeks, and it took several months for the toe to heal. The circumstances of that night still haunt me. The day after it happened, I found two windows unlocked on the first floor at the back of the house. At the time, there were just empty lots behind us, so someone could have come in that way without being seen. Our windows had no security system sensors on them, although that really doesn't seem to matter.

Over the course of six years, I woke up to see two men in the bedroom several times, and this was the third house where it had happened. Those are just the times when I had distinct memories of something happening. Each time, it felt like I had been drugged, and I could barely remember it. I always felt so groggy that I went back to sleep, even though I would later remember that there were strangers in the room, and I wondered why I was too tired to do anything about it. The closest thing I can compare it to is the feeling of coming out of anesthesia after surgery. This time was especially disturbing, not just because of my broken toe but because it made me think about the possibility that once Mark and I were drugged, one or both of these men may have told me to get out of bed and walk somewhere. What if they had done this before and I was just lucky enough not to injure myself? What in the world were they doing?

This house in City C was the first house where I had a locksmith install bolt locks on the inside of each exterior door. This is the type of lock that locks from the inside and has no key for entry on the exterior. As I said earlier, the day after this happened, I found two unlocked windows (double hung type) on the first floor. I can only assume that intruders came in when we were not there and unlocked the windows in preparation for this night. When we were gone from the house, intruders had entered many times when the security system was armed, and all the doors were locked.

As was true in City A and City B, there were numerous incidents that revealed that our house and my car were entered when we were not there. At this point, I had not filed any police reports because nothing was ever missing and there was no proof. Several times when I left the house, I locked the doorknob and the deadbolt on the door that led from the house to the garage. When I returned, only the doorknob was locked, which was easier to do since it didn't require a key to lock it. Sometimes the kitchen table was moved out of place slightly. Whoever was doing this was not always very careful. My computer was moved on several occasions. Light fixtures, phones and televisions were also moved slightly, cables loosened, etc. On occasion, window shades would be shut when I had left them open. I especially noticed this when I went to an appointment confirmed by telephone, such as a hair appointment or a medical appointment. I would say that during the years this has been going on, there have been hundreds of times that I found evidence of an intruder having been in the house.

One summer evening, Mark and Cindy went to go walk and jog at the outdoor track at the high school. They had been gone for about twenty minutes when I decided to ride my exercise bike for a while. After I was on the bike for a few minutes, I heard the chime sound (3 beeps) that our security system made when a door was opened! There was a keypad in our master bedroom, which is where my bike was, so I heard it clearly. At that point in time, we had become very diligent about making sure the doors were shut and locked, whether we were home or not. At first, I thought that Mark and Cindy must have come home earlier than I thought they would for some reason. I called out, but no one answered. I was upstairs at the end of the hall, but I headed downstairs to see what had happened. When I got downstairs, the doors were all shut, but the front door was unlocked. At that point, I couldn't see anyone walking or running down the street, so I don't know what happened. I walked all over the house to make sure no one had come in and was hiding somewhere. Instead, it seemed like someone had already been hiding in the house and had just left.

I don't know where this person went so quickly, but the doors were all closed, and one of the exterior doors had to have been opened to make the chime sound! As soon as Mark and Cindy returned home, I asked them if they had come back home about twenty minutes after they left, and they said no. Over the many years this has been going on, there have been numerous times when I suspected that one or more people were in the house while we were home. On that particular night, I can only guess that he (or she) was hiding under a bed, in a closet, or in the attic. He must have decided to leave the house at that point because he heard me riding my exercise bike and thought I wouldn't be able to get downstairs soon enough to see him.

Our home in City A did not have a security system. By the time we moved to City B, we had a monitored system. During our two and a half years there, the security company called several times to report trouble with our system. We received several calls in the middle of the night saying that they had a report that our system had switched to battery backup, meaning that the electricity was not working. I don't know exactly how the intruders bypassed the system in City B, but they did. I can only assume that it had to do with shutting off some or all of the electricity to our house.

However, I do know how they initially attempted to get around the system in City C. In December of

2000, I received a call from the security company that someone was tampering with our system. A tampering signal had been sent to the monitoring system regarding our wireless remote. The security company representative asked me to do a few tests from the keypad, and then she asked me about the wireless remote. I told her that we didn't have a wireless remote, but she was sure that they had issued one to us, and she sent a technician out. He found that our system had been set up to work with a wireless remote opener. The remote opener would disarm the system without the need for a code! The control box in the basement had come from the factory with that set to "off," and someone had to change it to "on" to work with a remote. The technician again disabled the remote function.

Both in City B and in City C, we continually had people tell us that they called our home number and got the sound of a fax machine. I even had it happen to me a few times when I had reason to call home. I could often hear someone else on the line, but at that time, the phone company had only found one illegal wiretap, or intercept, on our line. A few times, I hit the redial button for last number that called, and I got a number I had never called or even recognized! Since 1994, we have had way too many strange things happen with our phones.

In 2000, I updated my alumni information online for a university I attended. They were trying to get everyone to update their information for a new alumni directory. A few months later, I went online to confirm the information, and someone had changed my home phone number to what turned out to be a fax machine in New Jersey! I actually called the number, (908) XXX-XXXX, to see how there could have been such a mix-up, and a fax machine answered. I couldn't help but wonder if there was a connection to all the people who had tried to call us and got a fax machine. Anyone with my social security number could have logged on to my university information, and I know that my stalkers definitely had that, plus much more. I did check with the university, and they said they would never change someone's phone number.

About a year after we moved into our house, I noticed a leak under the kitchen sink. This was not an ordinary leak but obviously a man-made leak. Every time any water would go through the PVC pipe under the sink, some would drip out of a small hole in the side of the pipe. I called the plumber, and he said someone had to have made the hole with a drill because it wouldn't just appear like that. It was a perfectly round hole, and he said it would have to have been made by a very small drill bit. He asked if we were sure we had not done any work under the sink. It was almost comical to think that we would do some work under our kitchen sink and accidentally drill a perfect hole through our water pipe! I assured him we had not and that I had no idea how the hole appeared there, and I asked if he would please fix it. Of course I knew how the hole had appeared there, as it was a classic malicious act of our stalkers. I'm sure the stalkers were having a good laugh about it since things like that are how they amuse themselves.

In September, 2000, we bought a new SUV. I was the one who usually drove it. One day, I got in the car, and there was a single screw on the driver's side floor. I then noticed that the plastic molding around the driver's side dashboard looked like it had been removed. It looked the way it might look if someone removed the dashboard cover to install a CD player or put in a new radio. However, nothing like that had been done to this car. I know it did not look that way the last time I was in it. So why had someone taken the dashboard cover off on this car? At that point, I figured it had something to do with a hidden listening device or GPS. Somehow, people figured out where I was whenever I drove anywhere.

This same SUV was keyed along one side while it was still very new. The stalkers have been very consistent in making sure that any new cars we have brought or leased have been dinged and scratched several times during the first month or so. Damage and flat tires continued after that. Of course, these types of things can happen to anyone at any time, but we have had so many flat tires and damage to our vehicles since the stalking began that it is way too much to be just random mishaps.

In March, 2001, Mark, Cindy and I, as well as Mark's two brothers, all went to State D to visit Mark's parents in the City D area. One day, we made reservations by phone for dinner that night at a restaurant by the ocean. Just moments after we were seated, a man who I believe was Dr. Anthony Hanson walked in. He was with a woman, and they were seated at a nearby table. I had not seen him for several years, but if it wasn't him, it could have been his brother. He had the same build and the same hair color. It looked just like him. After dinner, I went to the restroom, and just as I came out of the stall to wash my hands, there was the tall, slender woman whom I felt I had seen several times before – in different cities! I was so surprised that for a moment, it seemed as if I had lost my ability to speak. I couldn't even figure out how to turn on the faucet. She just stood there and told me that she had just had the same problem when she was in the restroom earlier, and she turned on the faucet for me. I was in total shock and really couldn't speak. At that time, we were over a thousand miles from home, and two of the people I believed were involved in the stalking game were both at the same restaurant. I went back to our table, and we left a short while later. The man (probably Dr. Hanson) and the woman he was with left a minute before us, but they were waiting outside when we left. I have no idea why I didn't say anything to the woman in the restroom, but I always assume that if I say something, the person will completely deny that we have ever run into each other or met before. The scary thing here is that our reservations for dinner out that evening were made on the phone of Mark's parents, in their home. So, most likely, their phone or home was also bugged.

Things kept happening in our house. There was evidence of computer use, lights messed with, the door not double locked when we returned even though it had been double locked when we left, and a window shade closed when I had left it open. I wanted to confront the person I thought was stalking me, or at least the person I believed had somehow been involved from the start. Sometime in the fall of 2001, I called the home number for Dr. Anthony Hanson in City X. The number was in his wife's maiden name (Jones), but it showed up on the background check from the private investigator I had hired. I talked to his wife. She said he wasn't there at that time and asked if she could take a message. I told her my name and asked if it sounded familiar. She said no. I then asked her if she and/or her husband had been in the City C area in the past few years, and she refused to answer. She said I would have to ask her husband, and she wasn't going to answer any more questions. I said it was an easy question to answer; the answer was either "yes" or "no." She declined to answer.

The following day I called again, and I talked to Dr. Hanson. He denied having been in City C in the past twenty years, and he wondered why I would ask such a "cryptic" question. I told him that someone was spying on me or stalking me, and he said he didn't have any knowledge of it whatsoever. He seemed surprised that I had his phone number and asked me how I got the number. I didn't answer him. That was the end of the conversation, and I have never called there again. His unlisted phone number (listed only under his wife's maiden name) seems to fit my impression of him. He seems overly concerned with his own privacy, even though he is a medical doctor, and he has little or no concern for the privacy of anyone else.

It was May, 2002. Mark went to a city a few hours away to see Cindy compete in the state high school track tournament. I decided to stay home. They were gone all day Friday and got home very late Saturday night. On Friday, I went out to run errands and then came home for the evening. Sometime after midnight, I awoke to hear voices outside. The garage was right under the bedroom, and I later realized the voices were probably coming from there. I didn't get up at the time because I thought that it must be our neighbors out in their yard or coming home. On Saturday, I got in my car (the SUV) to do some shopping, and I started to back out of the garage when I realized one of my tires was completely flat! It had been fine when I returned on Friday. Of course, I would never be able to prove it. I had AAA put on my spare, and then I went to the tire store, where I had to spend most of Saturday waiting for my car. The AAA driver said he didn't see how I drove the car home from wherever I got the flat. They found a screw in the tire and were able to patch it. After having had this happen so many times, I felt so vulnerable and insecure. I was very sure at that point that the voices I had heard the night before were the people (probably the two men) jamming a screw into my tire in the garage.

One Saturday later that year, Mark, Cindy and I went to a large home show exhibition in downtown City C. We were probably there for a couple of hours. As we were working our way toward the exit, something caught my ear, and I turned around as we were walking. There was Anthony Hanson walking between two other men just several feet behind us! He immediately looked the other way and walked over to an exhibit. We kept walking and left. When we got out to our car (we drove my SUV), it had a big dent in one of the front doors. It looked more like someone had hit it with a hammer than a ding from a car door. Was that another random mishap?

CHAPTER FIVE

THE DISCOVERY OF GROUP STALKING

At some time in 2003, I was surfing the Internet for information on stalking. I knew what had been happening to me for several years, but I had no idea that the same types of things could possibly be happening to anyone else. Of course, I knew what stalking was, and I had read and heard about stalking situations the same as everyone else. These ranged from the stalking of the President of the United States to celebrity stalking, as well as the stalking of an individual by another known or unknown individual. The difference was that most of the stalking cases I had heard about were done by one individual. I couldn't piece together how I could be stalked by so many people. After reading everything I could, I thought I would never find any information on anything resembling what I was going through.

Then I came across a website (and eventually many websites and blogs) about a concept called "group stalking." It is actually referred to by many names, including gang stalking, organized stalking, multi-stalking, cause stalking, revenge stalking, and other terms. I think that the terms "group stalking" and "organized stalking" seem to be the most descriptive terms for this hate crime, at least as it relates to me. There is also a term called "stranger stalking." That term certainly applies to my situation as almost all of the people involved appear to be strangers.

For several days, I was in a state of disbelief and shock. After thinking that I was the victim of some unique and endless game thought up by one unknown person, I had now discovered that what I was going through was being experienced by countless people all over North America and elsewhere. I was upset that it had taken me so long to discover this. Although organized stalking is widespread and global, the majority of people are still not even aware of its existence. It is a crime that is not easy to prove, and it is underreported due to the target's fear of ridicule and embarrassment. Most people who try to report it to the authorities are met with skepticism and are often told that they should seek psychiatric help for their delusions. Very few people seem to readily believe it when they first hear about it. I'm fairly certain that I might have been in that category before it started happening to me.

It was shocking to read about all of the tactics used on the victims of organized stalking because I had experienced so many of them myself! All this time, I thought I was the only one going through this. This included home invasions, ongoing surveillance, street theater, vehicle entry, tampering and vandalism, telephone and computer sabotage and hacking, mail tampering, following and stalking me (us) everywhere we went, and on and on and on.

Another tactic that is often written about is how organized stalkers frequently attempt to recruit neighbors of the targets to help spy on them! They are in the perfect location to do that, and they could even help the stalkers monitor activities and conversations because they are close enough to do so. In some cases, the stalkers convince the neighbors to harass the target in some way or even to vandalize his or her home or property. One tactic they use is to research which neighbors don't really know the target that well. Then they tell them lies about some criminal activity in which the target is involved. They participate in what could legally be called "reputational slander." Other times, they might just need to offer the neighbor an "incentive" or ongoing payments to get them to cooperate. They often obtain financial background information on the neighbors. This would provide information on which neighbors might be more receptive to a bribe or an offer to keep close tabs on the target for ongoing payments.

I am curious as to whether neighbor recruitment has increased as gasoline prices have gone up. The literature on organized stalking says that this has been going on all along. The question is whether they have tried to enlist the help of a target's neighbors even more than they did in the past.

I already knew of the involvement of our next-door neighbor in City A and the neighbor across the street in City B. After reading about this, I began to think about other possible neighbor involvement. In both of the above situations, I am certain that these neighbors could hear inside our house. Did that mean that others, in every house we had lived, could do the same?

Now that I had found some resources, I was able to read about the sorts of people who might become targets of organized stalking. Some of the people who have been targeted have been identified as whistleblowers, political activists, or perceived enemies of a group or organization. Some of the "cause" stalking groups may target public officials or abortion workers. However, a large percentage of targeted individuals have no idea why they were selected. I fall into that category. If the organized stalking group has no real reason for targeting an individual, they will manufacture a lie about some crime the victim has committed and gotten away with. I have had many years to think about this, and I still have no idea why I was targeted. I believe I was probably in the wrong place at the wrong time.

There has also been much written about the sorts of people who would participate in organized stalking. There are behavioral professionals and many others far better qualified to comment on this than I am. However, I have come to some of my own conclusions in these past few years. One thing I read that made sense to me was that participants in organized stalking feel some sense of entitlement to their stalking pursuits. No matter what, they feel they are entitled to do whatever they want to do. This includes illegal home intrusions, breaking into vehicles, tapping phones, following targets everywhere they go, and basically almost anything else they decide to do. To me, that suggests that they feel no remorse for any of these deeds, and that sounds like a sociopath. I truly believe this is the case. I believe some of the participants have been persecuted in their own lives and have come to believe that they can do what they please to other people.

The people who join a stalking group are said by many to have low self-esteem. They are happy to be involved in a group with a united purpose, even if they are not even sure what the target has supposedly done. Most of what I have read suggests that the participants in a stalking group are often not even aware of the true identity of the "leader." Communication is almost always carried out by cell phone, text messaging, and the Internet. A participant may be notified to go "pick up" and follow a target whose car is currently parked in a certain parking lot. That is why a target will often notice an individual sitting in a nearby vehicle when they return to their vehicle in a parking lot. Obviously, there could be numerous other reasons why that person could be sitting in their car, but if it almost always happens, and that person almost always seems to start their car right after the target does, it begins to feel like more than a coincidence. I have had this happen to me hundreds of times, and some of them (the stalkers) are more discreet than others.

Over the years, I have asked myself many times if I could ever be convinced to participate in organized stalking. The answer has always been NO. I have not been able to think of a single situation in which I would participate. I believe in the Golden Rule of doing unto others as you would have them do unto you. It is not hard to live life with this belief. However, it is very hard to see how many people don't care what they do to others. As far as I can tell, organized stalkers go against the Golden Rule every day they wake up and participate in organized stalking activities. We are not talking about legitimate occasions when federal or local law enforcement personnel have court orders to wiretap a phone or to put surveillance on a suspect in a crime. We are talking about sociopathic criminals who get their jollies by harassing and spying on innocent people. I would put organized serial stalkers in the same category as serial rapists and murderers.

Please see the Appendixes for samples of some of the literature on organized stalking.

CHAPTER SIX

CONTACTING THE FBI IN CITY C

In 2003, I sent a report of our situation to the FBI in City C. It was basically the same information I had submitted previously with additional information about incidents that had happened since then. Of course, I used all the real names and locations. I addressed the envelope to Kent Martin, as he was listed as the "Special Agent in Charge" of the City C office at that time. In a follow-up call to their offices, I was told that they could not say if they received my information or not, but that it didn't matter because they didn't handle stalking cases. I was told to contact my local police department with any concerns. The name of the "Special Agent in Charge" is important for yet another coincidence that happened later.

CHAPTER SEVEN

2003 - 2005 CITY C

In 2002, we started building a house in a more rural area of the county where we lived. We moved into the house in early 2003. This move, like the others, did not stop the stalking. I had the security company pre-wire the house for a security system before we moved in. That was bypassed on numerous occasions. The security company technicians left a small open hole in the garage drywall to the left of the door to the house. It had something to do with not knowing if the basement directly below would be finished or not. When they came to activate the system, they finished the wiring for that door's sensor and screwed a plastic plate over the hole in the wall. Several weeks after we moved in, the builder came to the house to review some items that needed to be taken care of. We noticed that the weather stripping on the door from the garage was ripped at the bottom, about two inches up. The builder claimed that our security company did it since a door sensor was on that side. I later looked at it more closely, and when I pulled the weather stripping apart, I noticed a bundle of wires hidden behind the weather stripping. I pulled at them, and when I shut the door, the door chime did not sound. I jiggled the wires again, and the door chimed again. I tried this a few times, and each time I was able to disable and then enable the sensor for that door, all from some wires hidden in the weather stripping. When the door was shut from the garage side, I was still able to touch the wires.

I called the security company the following day and reported the situation. It was Tuesday, and we set up a service call for that Thursday so a service tech could see what I was talking about. I was gone from home most of Wednesday. When the service tech showed up on Thursday, I had not rechecked the weather stripping because I knew exactly what I needed to show him. However, when we went to look at it, the wires were gone! Completely gone! The weather stripping was indeed cut, and he agreed it looked as if someone had tampered with the box in the wall, but even he could not figure out how someone could rig something like I said. The drywall next to the plastic plate was soft, as if someone had made a slightly larger hole and then patched it. We later had the security company move the wiring for that door to the basement. That may have changed how they bypassed the system, but it did not stop them.

I decided to call the local law enforcement and at least file a report of an attempted break-in. An officer came out to the house and wrote up a report. He seemed as puzzled as everyone else I have told about this. He said he would have a car drive through more often for the next month. He was just doing his job, but I knew at that point that no one was going to realize the extent of what I was talking about unless I documented it. I have believed all along that the people involved in breaking into our homes have used vehicles identical to ours and have driven directly into the garage, probably shutting the garage door right away. I also believe that the person driving would have to look similar to Mark or me, at least from a distance, to ensure that a neighbor would not be suspicious. Once again, the unbelievable nature of this situation makes it easy not to want to believe it. The extent to which these people have gone makes it easy not to believe it.

Something that started happening almost imme-diately after we moved in was more cars driving by our house and around one or more of the cul-de-sac streets in the subdivision. Because this was a new area, still being developed, it was easy to see cars drive in, see where they drove, and see them leave. There is no way that so many people would drive way out there so often. When we first moved in, a different car would drive through the entire subdivision about every fifteen minutes, all day, every day. If I was looking, I would notice at least two an hour at all hours of the day. Most of the time they didn't drive slowly, as if they were looking at anything in particular, but they drove as if they were on a mission. One might expect a few cars a week, and maybe more on the weekends, but there were many more than that. Of course, with all the new houses being built, there was always a lot of construction traffic, but it was usually easy to distinguish the two.

We kept the same phone numbers at our new home. There did not appear to be any problems in transferring the numbers. The phone company was to stop the phone service at one house and start it the following day at the new house. When we started to use the phone at our new house, it was obvious that our line was somehow connected to or being used at another location. By coincidence, the other people were using their phone a lot, as we would come to find out that there had been a death in their family. The reason I know this is that I was talking on the phone when another phone started ringing in my ear. After so many rings, there was a third party on the line. I asked him what number he was calling, and he said he was calling the Miller family at "(999)999-9999." (It was not our number.) After I hung up, I called the phone company, and they sent a technician out. The technician researched the Millers' phone number and said they lived around a certain intersection in City C. He checked, and he found no possibility of any way it could have happened. He said our phone line and their phone line never went near one another! He told me that he traced our line all the way to the main station of the phone company.

I continued to hear people breathing on the phone, and after a few days, I called the Miller residence since I had written their phone number down from the earlier caller. We had experienced far too many strange things with our phones over the years not to follow up. I asked him if he was aware that his phone line and our phone line were somehow connected during the first few days of February. His answer was very odd. I expected him to say something about how strange it was and how he was glad it was fixed. Instead, he said that it never would have happened but that he had to go out of town for a funeral for a few days! He repeated himself, saying that it was all because he had to go out of town unexpectedly. So he was implying that we shared a phone line for a few days because he had to go out of town. Didn't he realize how bizarre that sounded? I wasn't sure what he meant, so I politely mentioned that it was a federal offense to illegally tap another person's phone. Again, his response was odd. He said they were planning to change phone companies in the next few weeks. He was either not very bright, or he thought a nonsensical reply would make him appear to be not so bright and force me to stop asking questions. I just let it go and said goodbye.

We still had our previous house on the market for a few months after we moved into this house. Our previous next-door neighbor's son was mowing our lawn that spring while the house was vacant. One day, Judy called me and said there was a spike in the back yard – the type that you can attach a dog chain to. She said her son almost ran over it with the mower. She asked me if the man who was working in the house might have had a dog there with him. I was completely puzzled, as no one should have been in the house unless there was a showing to a prospective buyer. She said that she saw a man coming and going for a few days, and he would let himself in and even drive into the garage. Just to make sure, I called our real estate agent to make sure they hadn't hired someone to do some work. He was as concerned as I was. He said that the house should be locked and no one should be in there unless there was a showing. My former neighbor, Judy, said that the man acted like he was supposed to be doing some work there, so she never even called me while it was going on. My suspicion is that he was removing hidden equipment and repairing anything else they had tampered with. I called another neighbor to see if she knew anything about the dog chain spike, but she hadn't noticed anything.

I returned home one day to find a small chip in a ceramic tile on the kitchen island counter top. Also, the wood steps from the garage to the house were all scratched up – paint was scratched off the front edges, as if something heavy had been dragged up the steps. There were smudges on the wall beside and behind the lower level television set. Also, the garage door opener was open (the door on the opener on the garage ceiling)! These are the types of things I had noticed for years. All of this happened while I was gone for several hours.

That day, I had gone to a luncheon where Julie Adams, a local news anchor, was the speaker. She was going to talk about her trip to Afghanistan. As I drove toward the luncheon location, a white Volvo station wagon appeared in front of me. It almost seemed that it had been at the side of the road before I turned the corner. I followed the car into the parking lot where the luncheon was held, and the woman who was driving waited to walk in with me. I had never met her before, but she looked familiar somehow. She was a tall, thin woman with very long, straight hair. As I talked with her and a few other women before the luncheon, she told us that she had spent about 30 years abroad. Her name was Wanda Nicholson, and she said she had been out of the country for several years where she taught English as a second language. She ended up telling us quite a lot about her life. She said they had recently returned to City C, and her husband worked for an engineering firm. She said she would be 50 years old the following year (2004) and that they had two small children. She also told Julie Adams that she had been in Afghanistan twenty some years earlier.

At the luncheon, Wanda Nicholson signed up for several activities and ended up joining the organization. That was how I got her address; it was published in the next newsletter. She had signed up for a potluck dinner that was to be held a few weeks after the luncheon. I had just signed up to go to the dinner before she did. I never said a word about this woman to anyone. Then, on the Saturday afternoon of the dinner, I mentioned Wanda to Mark and told him that something about her or her story didn't seem right, but I didn't know what it was. I just didn't believe all of her story, even if she had stood in front of a group of people and retold it. That was the first time I said anything about her.

When we arrived at the dinner, the hostess said that Wanda's husband had just called and they would not be able to make it. It was almost as if she had heard what I said, even though I said it in my own bedroom of my own home. Someone told me later that she never went to anything she signed up for. She never paid her dues and never joined the organization. Ordinarily, this might not be that surprising because there could be any number of reasons for this. However, I still had a strange feeling about her. One thing that made me uncomfortable was the fact that she was a tall, thin woman who looked like the same woman who kept showing up in my life. I am almost sure she was the same woman who lived in the short-term corporate apartment complex we lived in after moving to City C in late 1999, and I was fairly certain that she was the woman in the restroom of the ocean side restaurant in City D. Also, it almost seemed like she was waiting for me to show up at the luncheon that day. Why?

I asked a private investigator I had worked with to run a background check on her. The only thing I will mention at this time is that it showed she was originally from a distant state that was also in the background information of Anthony Hanson. This may or may not be relevant because it appeared that the organized stalker network was nationwide anyway.

One evening, Mark and I went out to dinner and then we ran an errand. Cindy was at a friend's house. It was dark when we returned home, and we saw the headlights of two cars driving near our house. One of them was speeding out of our driveway just as we entered our street! I had not armed the security system that evening because one of the door sensors had mysteriously stopped working. I did not want to take the time to read how to bypass one sensor, so I didn't arm it. I always lock the deadbolt on the door to the garage every single time I leave. This time, when I went to unlock the door, the deadbolt was not locked! What I had learned with this particular door was that it had to be shut very gently. If it was shut with too much force, you couldn't lock the deadbolt because the bolt wouldn't catch in the proper position. I figured out that whoever was leaving did not know that and spent too much time trying to lock the deadbolt. He or she finally left just before we got home, leaving the deadbolt unlocked.

This time, I noticed a few scuff marks on the dishwasher door. I looked under the sink, and for some reason, the electric cord for the dishwasher had been moved. It had been behind the PVC water pipe, out of the way, and now it was in front of it. Someone had to physically unplug it to do that. Again, why? Those are the kinds of details I notice. I had put everything away that we stored under the sink, and I know for sure that cord was moved. Also, one of the items on our list for the builder was the fact that our dishwasher and disposal often tripped the circuit switch in the basement. At that time, it had probably happened 4 or 5 times. It did not happen again after that night. I have no reason to believe that our intruders cared a bit about our home, so I have to think that once again, they must have done or undone something with the electric outlet under the sink. I can state with no uncertainty that someone was in our house that evening.

One afternoon in April, 2003, a white Volvo sedan followed me into Cindy's high school parking lot when I stopped by to see when Cindy would be finished with track practice. A woman was driving. After I talked to Cindy, I left to run an errand. The woman left right behind me. She did not seem to have a purpose for being in the parking lot. She never left her car, and she didn't pick up or drop off anyone. It seemed like she was just following me. Again, if this were an isolated event, I wouldn't have thought twice about it. But for years, I have had things like this happen over and over. It seems that there are many occasions where someone wants me to know they are following me.

After returning home that afternoon, I noticed that the upper cabinets over the sides of my stove seemed scratched in a few places. I climbed up on the counter, and I noticed that the window shade (which had been professionally installed a few months earlier) was loosened on one side, which it had not been before. There was a light in the ceiling above the stove. Were they tampering with the light or with the shade? Also, on that same day, there were a few pieces of attic insulation on the floor of the master closet, where the attic access was. No one had been up there, and there is no way that could have happened on its own! Again, I would bet my life on the fact that someone was in our house that day, but I had no real proof. I had begun to notice that on the days when it was apparent to me that there had been intruders in our house, I could recall a more obvious sense of being followed in my car while I was out. I believe that when they are planning to break in to the house, they make sure someone is watching me the whole time I am gone. I'm sure the same thing is true with my husband's car, but he is generally gone for much longer periods of time than I am.

One day, I was gone between 2:15 and 3:30 p.m. to run some errands. I armed the security system when I left. When I returned, even after such a short time, I found evidence that the attic access door in the master closet ceiling had once again been moved. Since I had found some attic insulation on the floor a few weeks earlier, I had just been looking at that door earlier in the day. There were also several paint shavings on the floor under the door. Again, I was sure someone had been there while I was gone.

On several occasions, I discovered that my computer had been tampered with. I found that my directories and files were different, the font had been changed, and my "Favorite Places" file had been deleted. Since I am the only one who ever uses my computer, I know that someone had messed with it.

One day in May, 2003, I was gone from 12:30 p.m. to 6:30 p.m. Someone was there without a doubt. The door threshold from the garage to the house was all scuffed up, and there was an extremely sticky substance in 3 places. It was not like that when I had left. I also found the same sticky substance in one of the bathroom sinks!

Our house had several tall, vaulted ceilings, and we had inspected them all very well before we moved in. The reason we had looked so closely was because a scaffold had shifted on some workers while they were painting the ceiling, and they made a few big gashes on one side of the ceiling. After it was repaired, we looked the entire ceiling over, and we found no other problems. The ceiling was fine when we moved in. One day, I happened to look up at the ceiling over the breakfast nook area and noticed a gash and a long scratch on the ceiling. They had not been there before, and I confirmed that with Mark. The angled ceiling was about 10 feet up at the place I'm talking about. No one had done any work or repairs of any kind, and it was not a stress crack. It looked like a ladder or something had been dragged along there. The only thing anyone could be trying to get to from that point would be the ceiling attachment of the light fixture over the table. I know that they had tampered with chandeliers in previous houses, but this one was about fourteen feet off the ground! They sure do like to mess with our light fixtures!

The cars continued to drive through this rather isolated subdivision in far greater numbers than would be normal. There were only 39 lots there, and it was somewhat out in the country. There were still days when cars would drive through every 15 to 30 minutes. These cars had no apparent purpose. They didn't drive as if they were interested in looking at available lots. I could see them drive in from the kitchen window, and then they would drive around two or three of the cul-de-sacs and leave.

I mentioned earlier that we have had a notable increase in small planes and helicopters flying directly over our homes. That is one of those things that I wouldn't have thought too much about were it not for all the organized stalking activities going on continuously. There was a day when we lived in this house that there was no doubt that our house was targeted. The houses in this somewhat rural area all had multi-acre lots, so there was a lot of open space between the homes. One day, when I was home alone, I suddenly heard an extremely loud noise. It sounded like an airplane. I was standing in the kitchen and ran to a large window to see what had happened. Just as I got to the window, a completely black airplane buzzed the roof of our house. It had obviously flown down low enough to be just yards above our house, and it was starting to fly up as soon as it was over our house. It happened very quickly, but I did get a good look at it. It was definitely some type of small plane, and I didn't see any color on it except solid black.

There was no doubt that the pilot meant to buzz low over our house, but I have no idea if it was just random or if it was connected to everything else.

Since it was so obviously aimed exclusively at our house, I really didn't think it was totally random. I called the closest municipal/executive airport in the area to report it and to see if I could get some information. The man I spoke to had no idea what might have happened. He said he had not seen any planes like that and asked if it might have been a helicopter. I assured him it was a plane of some sort, not a helicopter. He said the only thing he could think of was that it was a military aircraft. As to why it might have flown down so close to our house, he had no idea.

We also continued to have phone problems. At times, I could hear someone breathing on the phone, and we continued to have problems receiving calls at certain times. We had voicemail, yet some people said that they called and the phone just rang and rang and never went to voicemail. In those cases, we never heard the phone ring.

In July, 2003, I was gone from the house from 12:45 to 4:30 p.m. I took Cindy out for lunch after talking about where we were going as we drove there. Two women were waiting inside the restaurant. One was on a cell phone, and they seemed unusually interested in watching us walk in. The one woman continued to talk on her cell phone while we ordered and waited for our food. They watched us the whole time, and then they left. When we returned home later that afternoon, a counter barstool had been pulled out, and a cabinet door under my computer monitor was left slightly open. When I turned on my computer later that day, it said it had not been shut down properly.

In August, we drove to Colorado and had a whole caravan of stalker cars following us during the long car trip. Many of the cars had kids in them. Two or three times, as I casually looked out the car window at a car we passed, someone in the other car waved vigorously and smiled, as if they knew me. These types of things had happened before. One time, we were driving on an expressway somewhere when a kid in a car next to us kept motioning and pointing to us. He had some kind of radio or receiver, and he seemed to be yelling at his parents that he could hear us. They seemed to be trying to get him to stop talking. I guess he had heard our conversations for a while, and as they drove by our car, he realized it was us. Maybe it was Cindy he had heard talking, and when he saw her in the car, he thought she was the girl who had been talking. We had nothing in our car that would be transmitting our voices. However, I have known from the beginning that they continually hide some type of transmitting device in our cars. In that particular case, I don't know if they were part of the organized stalking and had their receiver set to pick up our car conversations, or if the boy found it accidentally. My guess is that they had it set to listen to us, but they hadn't told the kid what it was about.

We ended up staying at a lodge/condominium type place near Breckenridge, Colorado. We were followed everywhere we went for the whole trip. The day we were leaving, I picked up our room phone to make a call, and there was a man on the line describing OUR trip to someone! He was telling the other person where we ate, that we didn't eat any meals in our condo, and other things. I tried to say something, but as soon as I said a word, we were cut off. Another day, Cindy and I were sitting in the lobby for a few minutes as we waited to meet Mark. A man walked into the lobby and headed for the elevator. Just as he walked in and saw us, he started to loudly sing a song (an old song, but a classic) that I sometimes sing around the house as I am working, etc. Of course, that could be a coincidence, but in this case, I doubt it.

One morning, I found our garage door opener light on when I opened the door to the garage. It had not been on the night before. The electricity had also gone out for several seconds earlier that morning. I was going to play in a regularly scheduled bridge game that day, and I had talked about it on the phone. Those seem to be the days they break in – when I have a known appointment, especially when I schedule or discuss it on the phone. There was something they were getting ready for. When I returned home later that day, the counter stool was out again. Also, my desk chair was raised to a higher position than usual.

The same things continued to happen in the house while we were gone. Trim and walls and doors were scratched, locks were tampered with, and televisions, computers and light fixtures were tampered with.

In March of 2004, Mark, Cindy and I went to New York City over Cindy's spring break. We stayed in a large hotel. However, as large as it was, we kept seeing the same man again and again. He always seemed to be in the lobby as we were coming or going. He got on the same elevator that Cindy and I got on to go downstairs to breakfast one day. It seemed that he knew everywhere we were going and when. When we returned from sightseeing, there he was in the lobby. I assumed that at the very least he had our hotel room bugged. That would be the only way he could have known exactly when we were leaving and where we were going.

Organized stalking often seems to involve following the targets all over the country. It has been documented that they frequently do this. The main stalking group exists in the town or city where the target lives, but they have connections all over the country and use them as needed. I don't know exactly what their "connection" is since I don't know who is doing this, but I do know that they have had people follow and monitor us on every vacation we have taken. We have been targets in three different cities where we have lived in the U.S. When a target moves, they establish a new stalking group in the new city.

In April, a car with a man inside was parked just down the street from our house. He had been there for about an hour when I left at 6:30 p.m. to go pick up Cindy from school. She had something going on after school that day. I had talked to both Cindy and Mark about the time I would be leaving to pick her up. He started his car and followed me out of the subdivision when I left.

The attic access opening panel in our house had been sealed shut by paint. I had recently repainted it, and the not-quite-dry paint had stuck. I thought this was a good thing because I knew that if it became unstuck, that meant someone had purposely done it. It would have taken a bit of a shove to loosen it. We had earlier evidence that someone was going up there because there were pieces of insulation on the floor below on more than one occasion. When I returned home one day, the attic access opening was once again completely loose! I had just called a company and told them I would like someone to check out the attic area because it smelled very musty in the closet underneath it. There had been several hard rains prior to this. This company was going to be coming out the next week to clean up some water damage in our basement. I guess the phone call about having someone go up into the attic triggered something. Also on this day, the lock box I kept in my closet (the same closet where the attic access is) was unlocked. I always kept it locked.

One Saturday, I was out doing errands, and my last stop was the drug store. A man in a white station wagon followed me out of the parking lot. I didn't see him come out of the store, so I believe that he was already in his car in the parking lot. In his car, he followed me out of the parking lot and stayed right behind me. I changed lanes and slowed way down. I have become very uncomfortable about being followed after being stalked for so many years. As soon as I slowed down, he slowed down in the other lane. I had to almost come to a stop before he would finally drive ahead of me. I had such a strange feeling about him that I followed him from a distance. He went right to the house of Wanda Nicholson! She is the person who attended the luncheon I was at the year before and had appeared to be waiting for me. There was no doubt in my mind that he was now stalking me, just as Wanda Nicholson had. The main thing that made me suspicious was how he refused to go around me, even when I pulled over into the right-hand lane and slowed down. Most cars would zoom around someone like that. I believe he was Wanda's husband or significant other.

One day, Mark, Cindy and I had an appointment, which had been confirmed and discussed by phone. The house was entered while we were away for 3 hours. I had set a sort of trap, which had been disturbed while we were gone. This time, the light over the master shower/tub was very dirty. It looked like someone with dirty or greasy hands had handled the white metal shade around the light bulb. It was not like that before. Also, there were a few smudges on the side of the whirlpool tub, just below these lights. The light is 12 feet off the ground.

In the summer of 2004, I began to experience multiple health issues that required medical care. I was subsequently diagnosed with an autoimmune disease, which would eventually require testing, medications, and major surgery. Since that time, I have been diagnosed with other serious medical conditions, and I have had many other symptoms. Again, in order to protect our privacy, I do not wish to disclose the details. I will say that many of the symptoms related to my health issues are the same symptoms documented by many other victims of organized stalking and technological harassment. I have no family history of any of these conditions.

The medical professionals have not been able to determine what caused all of these health issues, but I can and do blame the stalkers. At the very least, the stress of having been stalked 24/7/365 for the past ten years was a factor! Organized stalkers are sociopaths; many times, I have wondered about and suspected that it was more than stress. All I know is that I was a healthy woman before all of this started, and now I'm not. My medical condition is something I will have to deal with for the rest of my life. The stalkers have been entering our homes and cars on a very regular basis since 1994, and there is no way to know what physical atrocities they have committed, what they might have tampered with, or to what extent I have been subjected to technological harassment.

A few weeks later, I returned to an imaging center for some additional tests related to my illness. The door to the imaging center had several steps leading to it. As I was approaching the steps, I noticed a man standing at the top, and he appeared to be using a cell phone. Then, as I started up the steps, he held the phone toward me and took a picture or a video of me! I was shocked that he would do that, but before I could even think what to do, he put the camera phone away and started quickly walking away in the opposite direction. He did not seem at all ashamed of what he was doing; rather, he appeared to be in a hurry to take the picture or video and leave. It was not the first nor the last time I have had that happen, but he was very intentional and obvious. He had to have known my schedule and exactly where I would be walking. As I have said before, I am not a celebrity – just an ordinary person who has become the stalking victim of some very disturbed people. This was not a normal thing to happen to an ordinary person. Although the parking lot was rather full, there was no one else walking up those stairs or even near the door at that time. He was obviously pointing a cell phone camera at me, and he appeared to take a picture. How very odd.

Over the course of a few months, for some unknown reason I was continually followed around stores by different people. It is hard to understand what would motivate a person to agree to do that, but I can't believe anyone would do it without being compensated in some way. First, a man followed me all over a department store. Once you have been a stalking victim long enough, you develop a sort of sixth sense about being followed. I am the first to say that sometimes, when it appears that someone is following you, they really aren't. However, most times when it appears that way, they really are. These men would stay a certain distance from me but never be out of my sight if I looked around. I never saw any of them buy anything, and they would usually disappear when I left, or even leave at the same time I did.

Within a few weeks, it happened at a Wal-Mart and at another department store. At Wal-Mart, it was hard not to notice. A man seemed to follow me at a bit of a distance as I entered the store. I took a cart, and he stalled a little while I did that. Then he proceeded to follow me from aisle to aisle, wherever I went, never looking me in the face. He pretended to look at merchandise close to wherever I was looking. When I went to check out, he left the store without buying anything. A man at the JCPenney store parked next to me and then followed me all over the store. I was actually returning an item, and then I looked around for a few minutes. He bought nothing and left when I left.

One day, I was in an optical shop when a man pulled up outside, double parked, jumped out of his car, and came inside. He looked around until he saw me, looked at me for a moment, and left. I watched as he got into his car and made an immediate cell phone call and drove away. How odd.

The research on organized stalking says that they do things like this to sensitize the targets to these activities so they will want to stop doing them. It is also a way of continuing to remind the targets that they are being watched. So, for some reason, they wanted to remind me that I was still being watched at all times. I already knew that. Every time I go to a store, at least one or more stalkers are there within a short time. They usually seem to want to see what I am buying or what I have in my cart. Sometimes, they seem to want to get close enough to bump into my cart. If it is a large store, like Target, they seem to hang around the checkout lanes if they think I am about ready to leave. They act like they are looking at some merchandise near the checkout lanes, but they keep giving quick looks in my direction, as if to see my next move. Then they inevitably get in line behind me. I assume this is so they can report on what items I bought and maybe how much I spent.

This sort of thing has happened since the stalking started. Again, all I can say is this: "How pathetic." One time, several years ago, I spotted a guy that I was sure was one of the group stalkers. He was hanging out near the checkout lanes and glancing at me every few seconds. When I reached a checkout lane and started to put my purchases on the counter, he immediately walked over and got in line behind me. I looked around and saw two or three open lanes with no one in line, so I pleasantly said to him, "There are two checkout lanes with no one waiting right there." Then I kept putting my items on the counter. He seemed kind of surprised, but he did walk over to the next checkout lane.

In December, 2004, Mark found a completely flat tire on his car in the garage. It had not been like that when he drove it home the night before. AAA put on the spare, and the tire store found a puncture hole, which they were able to patch. He had just bought four new tires for his car, and he ended up having three flat tires in the next six months.

CHAPTER EIGHT

2005 – PRESENT: CITY C

In March of 2005, we made an offer on a house as we had decided to move. After making the offer but before the closing, someone vandalized the empty house we were going to buy. The intruder(s) tampered with an electrical outlet in the front hall and tore off some floor trim and drywall in the front hall. The salesperson said no one had been authorized to do any work there, so they had everything repaired and didn't even tell us about it until after the closing. That was the first we knew about it. We later discovered that someone had also made a large hole in the exterior stucco of the house!

A month after we moved in, we were all away from home for several hours. Upon returning, I noticed a sprinkling of drywall dust on the carpet in the living room. It had not been there before we left, as it was fairly obvious, but there was no indication of where it had come from. We had spackle and extra wall paint in the basement, so if a hole had been made in the wall, it could have been patched and dried by the time we returned home. I know what I saw, but not why it might have happened. After all these years, I assumed that they needed to put something inside or take something out of the wall for some reason. Just ten days before, we had the locks replaced with higher quality locks. The only way I can imagine that they could get in was to pay off Martin the locksmith for an extra key. I'm sure they have done that on several occasions. There was no sign of forced entry.

Right after we were gone for most of the day, I noticed a few other things. Once again, the attic access door had been moved. They go up in our attics a lot! Also, I had called the lighting store that had supplied our light fixtures and ceiling fans. I asked for a service call to take care of a few issues. One thing I described was a ceiling fan that was excessively shaking when we ran it. They said it might need to be balanced, and their technician would look at it when he came out the following week. However, while we were gone for the day, the fan was mysteriously fixed. Not only did it no longer shake, but the fan now spun in the opposite direction. This would have required someone to get up on a ladder to flip a switch. The switch is about ten feet up from the ground. Since it was May and somewhat warm, the fan had been set to spin so the air would come down. It was now spinning in the opposite direction. Now, after all the years the stalkers have been in my life, I have never known them to do anything helpful to us. So, while they were in our attic and messing with airspace between our walls, it appeared that they also fixed that ceiling fan. That leads me to the conclusion that they didn't want a lighting store technician messing with that fan for some reason.

In September, 2005, I got a new car. The first month I drove it, the right front door was dinged three times. The first two dings were done before it even had a permanent license plate on it. I can't even imagine the mentality of people who waste their time deciding who will make the next ding in a target's car door. I believe the stalkers think they are sending a message of some sort, but it is difficult to try to figure out what a sociopath is thinking.

The following month, I noticed that the right side of my car's dashboard had a light dusting of a white powdery substance over the airbag opening. I knew that the passenger side front airbag was under there, but someone would have to have taken the airbag compartment apart to get to that. I was told that the airbags have a powder all over them, so I wondered if that was what it was. This was the second time this had happened in that car. I never found out what it was, and I completely cleaned the dashboard off. The only explanation I have is that someone opened the airbag compartment to remove or place something under there. I know that they have been able to somehow hide a GPS transmitter and a voice transmitter in every car we have had since 1994, so I assume it was something to do with that. Obviously, they don't really care if the airbag would actually work in an accident.

A few weeks later, I noticed a man driving by our house while holding something out of his car window, pointed toward our house. He only aimed it at our house, and then he put it back inside his car. He then turned around in a neighbor's driveway and made a cell phone call as he was leaving the area.

One day, I drove by the house of Wanda Nicholson on my way home from an appointment. From where I was, driving by her house was not out of the way to my house. I had done that on a few occasions (maybe twice in the past year and a half), as I had a strong feeling that she and her husband were somehow involved in stalking me. Just as I drove by, she was leaving her house, and it appeared that she had two children with her. I turned around and followed her from a distance. She went to a nearby soccer field, where there were already many people arriving. The parking lot was packed. She must have known I was there because she seemed quite unsure of what to do. I found a parking spot a few spaces from her and pulled in.

The only way she should have remembered me was from the club luncheon we both attended a year and a half before. I had a different car, and it would have been difficult for her to know who was even in my car unless she knew what my current car looked like. She seemed completely perplexed about what to do. She and the children stayed in the car for a long time, and I simply stayed in my car. I wanted to see her again to confirm that she was the same woman I had met at the luncheon. She finally got out, and they walked over to a soccer field. It was the same woman, Wanda Nicholson.

It certainly could not be that she was frightened of me. If she is part of this stalking game, as I suspect, then she knows very well that I am not a physical threat to anyone. Rather, I think she was embarrassed or ashamed that her target was so close and had followed HER. At most, she might have been concerned that I would ask her a pointed question in front of her children. For a stalking victim, trying to figure out what is going on is a full-time endeavor.

There were more signs of intruders in the house while we were out. The dishwasher settings were reset to the default settings, which happens only when the electricity to that appliance is shut off for some reason. There was a glob of paint on the master bath floor, and there were spots in the whirlpool bathtub, which is never used, as if a ladder was placed in there to get to the light fixture on the ceiling above. The control panel over the wall oven was tampered with and loosened. I had to call GE since it was under warranty. He tightened the control panel, which is separate from the oven. A month later, it happened again! The GE repairman came out again, and he said that somehow, the frame behind the control panel had been bent and it would never fit the same. It didn't really matter because thanks to whoever had been tampering with the control panel, the oven stopped working, and we had to have it replaced! Within a short period of time, the control panel on the new oven was also loosened and tampered with.

Sabotaging or damaging the target's appliances, electronics, and vehicles is one of their common tactics. So, if they aren't trying to hide something somewhere, they are just outright damaging things. Since all of this started, we have spent thousands of dollars on repairs to home appliances and cars as well as other home repairs. Since everyone has some ongoing repairs to deal with, it is not possible to say exactly how many can be blamed on the organized stalkers, but I would guess it could be at least half.

We have a planned service agreement for our heating and air conditioning systems. They come out twice a year and thoroughly check out the systems. Just recently, the HVAC technician found that one of the bolts securing the blower motor in our furnace had come completely out, and the other three were loose! He seemed puzzled because he was the same technician who had checked the system 6 months earlier. He asked me if anyone else had opened the furnace for any reason because he didn't see how one bolt could fall out and three could become loose in that period of time. He said it would be almost impossible. He went on to say that if he hadn't caught it, the motor would have eventually burned out and it would cost several hundred dollars to replace. Of course, I didn't know how to respond. I have read that the furnace is one of the favorite appliances for organized stalkers to mess with.

The previous time the HVAC technician had been to our house, he found that the firebox door had been put on the furnace upside down. He had asked me if we had taken it off for any reason. I told him we had never touched it. He said that none of their technicians would have installed it that way because they all knew how the door was installed. He said it didn't even go on that easily upside down, so someone would have had to force it on. When he found the loose bolts this last time here, I wondered what they had previously done to the furnace.

We have also had several plumbing-related problems in the past several months that required several hundred dollars in repairs. All of these are unusual things to happen to plumbing equipment that is only three years old. I believe all of these issues could have been, and probably were, created by the stalkers.

It makes me sick that someone capable of doing these things is continuing to enter our home. What is really sad is that knowing it upsets me is exactly what they are looking for. It would probably get a smile out of them. It seems to me that the current stalkers are getting more and more evil and vindictive as time goes by. The only explanation I have is that I am more vocal about how much I despise them, and in the beginning, I didn't even know what was going on. Obviously, there are different groups of organized stalkers in different cities. I also suspect that the tactics and types of harassment vary some. We have lived in City C since late 1999. I can only guess that some of the group players and leaders have changed over the years, too. I know it is at least safe to say that they are all disturbed sociopaths.

In January, 2006, I had a doctor's appointment at a medical office building. I checked in with the receptionist and went down the hall to the restroom. When I came out of the stall, there was a tall woman standing there. She definitely looked like one of the same tall women I continue to see at various places all over the country. She just stared at me for a few seconds and then went into the stall.

One evening, Mark and I were going to meet a friend at a restaurant for dinner. Our friend was from out of town, but he was in City C for business. He was going to meet us at the restaurant, and Mark and I had a few phone conversations that day concerning the time and place we would all meet. Mark and I drove together, and he dropped me off at the door of the restaurant so I could put our name on the list. We had not made reservations. It was quite crowded that night. The parking lot was very full, and there were people waiting inside when I walked in. I walked up to the desk where they took names and requested a table for three. The man at the desk said they could seat us right away, but I said the other two were not there yet and that I would wait for them. He said, "That's okay; I'll show you to your table, and when the others arrive, I'll send them back." I sort of described Mark and our friend and walked to the table with him. I was happy to get a table so quickly because it was so crowded, and our table was the only empty table that I could see! It had appeared to me that there were people waiting for tables when I walked in.

As soon as I sat down and glanced around, I saw the two women that I had seen on so many other occasions. I am 95% sure it was them. They were sitting next to each other at a booth, just several feet away, looking directly at our table. I was about to get up and leave, but Mark came to the table at just that moment and sat down. I would not have been able to say anything to him without the two of them hearing. Even if I had been able to communicate with him, I was afraid it would create a small scene just as our friend arrived. Once we were all there, I tried to ignore them, although they both frequently stared at our table the entire time. I still have no idea who they are or what their motivation is, but I believe they are somehow involved with the organized stalking. They look somewhat different every time I see them, yet there is something about them that makes me fairly certain they are the same people. I was left wondering if someone had "convinced" the guy at the front desk to save that table just for us or if this was just another coincidence.

In May, we had another day of street theater when I went with Cindy to the DMV to get a license plate for her car. She and I had talked about our plans that morning as far as where we would be going and when we would be leaving. You are supposed to take a number from a machine as you walk into this DMV, and it isn't unusual to have a fairly long wait. The man at the front counter initially called our number right away so he could make sure we had the proper documentation, etc. He then told us to wait for our number to be called. The place was especially crowded that day. All the chairs were taken, and many people were sitting on the floor.

As I looked around, it seemed that there were many people there who had no paperwork with them and didn't even appear to be holding a number. They seemed to be watching us a little too closely, too. After waiting for about an hour, they were getting close to our number. We were watching a machine on the wall, which showed the number being called, and we were also listening as they called the numbers. They called the number before ours, and we stood up, ready to go to whichever window called us next. Then, they completely skipped our number – after waiting for over an hour, they went right on to the next number!

After twelve years of things like this happening, I knew that someone had enlisted the help of one of the DMV employees to provide this street theater entertainment. We waited for about an hour, during which all the people who had no paperwork or numbers in their hands (probably 20 or 30 people) continued to sit in their chairs. Since the numbers are called in sequence, if they had been there for any type of business, they would have had their numbers called before us because they were all there before us. What is amazing to me is to think of the type of people who would do this. How many people have the time or inclination to go waste an afternoon at the DMV so they can watch the reaction of a woman and her daughter when their number is skipped after an hour of waiting? They seem to lead pretty pathetic lives. Supposedly, they get some kind of incredible satisfaction out of street theater like this.

I eventually got the attention of the man behind the front counter (probably the person who didn't put our number in to begin with), and he rudely accused us of not paying attention when they called our number. Both Cindy and I told him that our number had never been called. He continued to insist he was right, but he did finally put our number back in the system. If I had to guess, I would say he was the one who cooperated with the stalkers. When we finally got to the counter to request a license plate, I told the clerk what had happened. She was clueless and said that she and another woman had been called in to work at the last minute when the waiting area became so full two hours earlier. She said she had never seen so many people in the waiting area.

Another rather odd thing occurred during all of this, and I wasn't sure what to make of it while it was happening. About 10 or 15 minutes before they would have called our number, several men walked into the DMV, and none of them went to the front counter or took a number. Instead, they stood along a wall, a few of them with their arms folded. They looked to me like possible law enforcement people. They looked rather serious and seemed to be observing the entire waiting area. I have become so used to having strange things happen when I'm out that I just chalked it up to yet another incident about which I would not have a clue.

The only plausible explanation I could think of is that law enforcement was notified because there was such a very large crowd of people in the waiting area that day, and an observant patron or employee suspected something might be going on because so many people did not appear to be there to conduct any business. If one of these men had approached one of the stalker group members to ask why they were there, I'm sure they would have said something like they were supposed to meet someone there, and the person had not shown up yet. From what I have read, every stalker gang member is always supposed to have an explanation for why they are somewhere – why they are sitting in their car in a parking lot, why they are driving a certain route, etc.

However, just as on the flight several years before, it is entirely possible that these men were also part of the organized stalking group. Maybe they were there to see how the street theater prank turned out! That is a scary thought since they certainly could have passed for law enforcement agents of some sort. What was going on?

A few weeks later, the doorbell rang on a Sunday in the late afternoon. It was Memorial Day weekend, and we were about to put something on the grill for dinner. I was in the kitchen preparing for dinner when I went to answer the door. A woman identified herself as Sandra Martin, and she showed me her identification, which happened to be an FBI Identification Card. She explained that she and her husband had tried to call first, but we were not home, so she decided to stop by in person. She said that they were considering buying our previous house, and they were trying to get some additional information on it.

We had actually ended up selling the house back to the builder because of multiple problems with water continually coming into the finished area of our basement. We had moved out over a year before, and I assumed that the builder had found and fixed all the problems and repaired the damage caused by the water. She really just wanted to know what had been done before we moved out and whether we could supply any additional information about the water infiltration problem. Understandably, they wanted to make sure there were no more problems.

Sandra Martin mentioned that her husband, Kent, also worked for the FBI. I did not get the connection immediately, although I did think that the name sounded familiar for some reason. I ended up talking to her again a few months later about something else to do with the house. She told me they had decided to buy it, and it was then that I remembered the name "Kent Martin." He was the Special Agent in Charge of the FBI Office when I had sent in my letter and request for help three years earlier. I wrote the letter while living in the house they were buying. Sandra had mentioned his current position, which was a different one than he had previously held at the time I sent my letter.

I'm not saying that my 2003 letter/complaint sent to the FBI in City C was investigated and that the

Martins knew who we were. However, in a city with a 2007 greater metropolitan area population of nearly 2 million people, it certainly was another coincidence.

Another day, I ran some errands and then went to a small shopping center to look for a few things. As I parked my car, a car with a man driving and a woman passenger parked near me. They followed me into a home décor store, and they got a cart, as I did. They seemed to follow me around the store, but they put nothing in their cart. I believe they finally put a few items in their cart and continued to go wherever I went. I turned around to go another way, and the woman seemed to purposely push her cart into mine. She apologized, and I also said I was sorry. This has happened several times before – I would be shopping somewhere with a cart, and someone seems to "accidentally" ram their cart into mine. It has been written that this is a favorite tactic of these stalker groups!

These two people continued to follow me, so I decided to take a while looking at some more merchandise, hoping they would leave. They hovered around the checkout lanes, and I stayed in one place, looking at something. I finally glanced up, and they looked at me, left their cart with the one or two items in it, and left the store. It was as if they had no intention of buying anything; they were just there to follow and possibly torment me. These types of things have been going on all these years, over and over.

One day, I went to a doctor's appointment, which was located in a hospital complex. As I walked into the medical building, a woman who was sitting on a chair near the revolving door entrance held up her cell phone toward me and appeared to be recording a video of me. This wasn't the first time this had happened, but I noticed it because it was so obvious that she was targeting me for her picture(s). She had to have known that I would be walking in through those doors at that time. Another strange thing was yet to happen that day, after my appointment with the doctor.

I had to stop by the lab on my way out to have some blood drawn for lab work. There had been a long wait in the doctor's waiting room, so it had probably been an hour and a half since I had first walked into the building. As I checked in with the front desk at the lab, the woman at the desk said that a woman who looked just like me had just stopped by there to ask a question. She went on to say that she was wearing the same exact outfit, and she had the same hair color and style as I did. She said that she could have been my twin! She then repeated it as if it were the most amazing thing that had ever happened. I wondered if there was any connection to the woman who took my picture as I walked in the door. Why would anyone do that? Had the look-alike woman wanted to run into me to see my reaction? Once again, how very odd!

I received a call one day from an auto body shop, and the man said he was returning my call. I told him I hadn't called him, and he repeated my number. He correctly stated my number and said it had shown up on his caller ID earlier that day. I have no idea how that could happen unless someone was somehow using our number in another location. I have suspected that for a long time. Many times, I have been home alone with no phone in use anywhere, and the "line in use" light would be lit up on one of our phones. I have checked other things it could be (computer, security company line check, etc.), but it was not any of those. We do not have a dialup connection for our computer. When I picked up the receiver when the "line in use" light was lit up, there was no dial tone, but it would eventually return.

There are also continual strange things that happen with our cell phones. One day, I called Mark's cell phone from my cell phone while I was at home and he was at his office. He didn't answer, and as it was going to his voicemail message, I heard a man's voice talking as if he were talking to a room of several people. It was not "cross talk," as it didn't appear to be a phone conversation. Instead, it was as if he was intercepting my call and had not hung up because he was waiting to see if I said anything else. I reported the incident to the cell phone company, and they were interested in what might have happened.

A technician/investigator called me (on my cell phone) and said they checked out the call in question. He told me that it was very strange because my call "pinged" off a tower many miles from where our cell phones were at that time. He called me to make sure I was really at my home when I called my husband. He couldn't understand how that could happen. I asked if maybe someone could have cloned one of our phones or intercepted our call. He was only interested in the distant cell tower, as he couldn't explain it. Soon, two technicians drove up to our house, and they called and told me that they were going to try to duplicate the situation. They asked me not to use my cell phone as long as I saw them outside in front of our house. They stayed for about 45 minutes and then left. Since they informed me about what they were doing over my cell phone, anyone tampering with our phones could have temporarily undone whatever they did. Any conclusions they came to were never shared with us.

Just after 1:00 a.m. one night in July, 2007, we were awakened by an extremely loud noise, which came from outside the house. Mark was out of town on business, and I was sound asleep. Cindy was asleep in her room. There was a vehicle that must have stopped on the street behind us. There is an open area between two houses on that street that is directly in line with our bedroom window. After the very loud blast or bang woke me up, I saw a blue beam of light directed at our bedroom window. Although the window coverings on the windows were all closed, I could still see the light. The vehicle took off before I could get out of bed to see it. The stalkers seem to prefer to do some of their evil deeds when Mark is out of town, and they always seem to know everything about our schedules.

There have been numerous times since 2005 that a vehicle has stopped in that spot and seemed to shoot something toward our bedroom windows. If they actually pull into our rear neighbor's driveway, they are even closer to the back of our house, and their headlights shine through our bedroom windows even with the shutters completely closed. Sometimes I have felt like I received some sort of shock while lying in bed, and other times it has sounded like something was aimed at the house or windows and caused a loud noise when it hit it. The loud blast that night in July was unique. It really sounded like a bomb. I have no idea what the noise had to do with the blue light. These people are perverse and dangerous.

The fact that people have pulled into our rear neighbor's driveway on several occasions, usually in the middle of the night, is one of several reasons why I seriously wonder about these people. I never had any experiences with all the exterior loud noises, sounds (weapons?) and lights being shined into our windows until we moved to this house. Sometimes, a car has driven into the driveway behind us and just sat there with their bright lights shining toward our bedroom windows. Whenever I get out of bed to peek out the window, the car backs up and leaves.

The man living there, Adam Sloan, was a frequent smoker for many months after we moved in. He seemed to do all of his smoking on his back deck, always looking straight at our house as if he were looking in our windows. He would often lean on his deck railing and just stare at our house. It made me somewhat uncomfortable, but I never said anything to anyone. I usually adjusted the shutters so that he wouldn't be able to see in that easily.

One day, Cindy walked by and saw him out there. She commented to me what a creep she thought he was; he seemed to be out on his deck smoking cigarettes and staring at our house all the time. All our windows and doors were shut at the time, and he couldn't possibly have heard us, but we have never seen him smoking out there since then. Unless this was another coincidence, his wife, Jean, would have to have told him what we said when he went back in the house. Maybe he is still out there at night, and he goes out his front door to smoke during the day.

If there is such a thing as a type of person who would be willing to take money to spy on his (or her) neighbor, I believe that Adam and Jean Sloan could be that type. I am not surprised that Daniel Lloyd and John Vinson could be involved, either. No doubt it depends on what story the stalkers are telling them.

Three days before that incident in July, I made a note that all day long, there were cars driving by our house with the driver holding something out his window, aimed at our house. There were no sounds associated with it, just a strange number of cars all doing the same thing.

For a while, we were without surveillance cameras, and of course the stalkers knew that. They seem to make it their business to know everything about us. The home intrusions started up again. There were many intrusions during this time. One day, I came home and saw evidence that someone had been in the house while I was gone. I have a theory that there must be at least one of the intruders who hides in the house for periods of time. It is the only explanation for how someone could be in the house while we are sleeping because there are one-sided bolt locks on the doors, and we lock them at night. Either that, or there is another mysterious way of entering the house that we don't know about. We have an attic and an above-ceiling crawlspace over some of the finished lower level. It is possible that someone could hide in either of those places. I just don't know.

The one crawlspace I referred to is about 18 to 20 inches high, and it goes over Cindy's bedroom. Around the end of the year in 2007, Cindy was sitting in her room when all of a sudden her ceiling light fixture (the glass globe part) fell from the ceiling onto the floor and broke. The strange thing about that is that the bulbs in that fixture had never been changed, and the light fixture globe had never been removed since we moved in. Something had loosened it to the point that it fell from the ceiling. A few weeks earlier, I had been in her room, and I thought the globe looked like it was sort of crooked on the base of the fixture. However, since Cindy is away at college much of the time, I didn't remember ever changing the bulbs in that light. I just left it alone, figuring that it had been that way all along and it would be better not to bother it. After it fell, of course, I wish I had. Now I'm wondering what could have changed or compromised that fixture. It had to have been someone up on a ladder in the bedroom or over the ceiling in the crawlspace. I confirmed with

Cindy and Mark that neither of them had done anything to the light, and they had not. Another mystery, another light fixture tampered with.

I have often asked myself why ANYONE would go to such trouble and suffer such personal discomfort just to hide in an attic or crawlspace. All of that, just to continue the organized stalking activities? It doesn't make any sense. As I think about the numerous times I have sensed the intruders in the house at night while we were there, it makes me wonder if the organized stalking activities are a part of something even more heinous. The only thing I can think of is unauthorized medical research. It would certainly account for some of my continual health issues.

Neither Mark nor I fit any of the common criteria for most organized stalking targets. Maybe the organized stalking is being carried out in conjunction with physical and technological harassment or research. Since these tactics are so common in organized stalking, it is a possibility. I can't think of any other explanation for all the intrusions and the two men in my bedroom on numerous occasions. I now have many symptoms of this type of abuse. As bizarre as it sounds, being selected for nonconsensual research seems more plausible than other options. Having been such a trusting person for most of my life, it is inconceivable to me that this could happen.

There was something else I began to notice in this house. I have found several perfectly formed pinholes in both the wood trim and the drywall all over the house. The first one I found by accident, and since then, I have noticed several others. They don't stand out that much, so I think you would almost have to catch them by accident. The size is about the size of the very smallest drill bit one could buy for an electric drill. They remind me of the small, perfectly round hole the plumber found in the PVC pipe below our sink in 2000. I have actually taken a long jewelry stick pin I have, and it goes all the way straight into these holes. That makes me think they were not something that happened by chance. The pin has not seemed to hit anything, so I'm not yet sure what they are. I have covered several of the holes with a little bit of spackle. Very odd. I always figured the obviously man-made hole in the plumbing pipe was a malicious act of the stalkers. I suppose these could be the same, or they might be something else.

Something else I have continued to see in this house, as I have in others, is evidence of the removal of light switch and electric outlet cover plates. Sometimes there has been drywall dust on the floor beneath, and other times they just aren't replaced in the same manner in which they were originally installed. There have been some instances of obvious paint touchups at the edge of the plate.

One Saturday morning, I woke up with a large dark purple bruise on my inner forearm. It looked like it had a puncture mark in the middle of it. I have no idea how I got it, but it looked like the sort of bruise I sometimes get after having blood drawn. Instead of being in the crook of my elbow, it was in the middle of my right inner forearm. It was also somewhat painful, and it took several days to go away. I had not had any blood drawn recently, and that isn't the location they usually use anyway. I had no proof that anything happened and no recollection of what happened while I was sleeping, but that is usually the case.

In October, 2007, I believe I was targeted to be involved in an auto accident that failed. I was driving to a prearranged appointment, scheduled by phone, to a location at least 30 minutes from my home. I had driven there before, and I always took the same route. When I was a few miles from my destination, I noticed a maroon sedan pull out from a parking spot, and he stayed fairly close behind me. The street was four lanes wide. There were two in each direction because parking is allowed in the curb lane at certain times of day. The maroon car stayed behind me for a few miles, and I was approaching an intersection with a traffic light.

I noticed an older model white car stopped to my right in the parking lane, and there were people in it. There were also two men standing on the sidewalk near the back of the white car. The maroon car stayed close behind me. Then, just as I was approaching the left side of the white car, the two men pounded on his trunk lid and yelled "NOW!" He immediately pulled out, and I looked at him and he looked right at me. Luck was with me at that moment. I pulled over in the middle of the intersection (which was clear) in order to let him get ahead of me. I'm sure he meant to hit my car, but it didn't work! It was so obvious, and I think the driver of the white car was surprised when I moved out of his way. The place I was going was a few more blocks down the street. The white car was now in front of me, and the maroon car was behind me, and we all turned left at the same place. The white car turned into a bank parking lot, and I kept going. I slowed down and looked in my rearview mirror to see where the maroon car went. He pulled up right next to the white car in the bank parking lot! I had a feeling that they were together on this accident setup, and I'm sure they would have tried to say it was my fault somehow. The maroon car would have been their witness.

It seemed like an extreme way to try to mess up my day or pull some sort of accident scam. They were most likely involved with the organized stalkers because I was too far from home, and they seemed to know what my car looked like and exactly when I would be driving by a particular spot. In setups like this, the stalkers supposedly use several cars, which trade off as they follow a target to his or her destination.

A few weeks later, Mark and I parked in a fairly empty parking lot while we were out for the evening. When we returned to the car, some air had been let out of two of the tires, certain internal settings had been changed in the car, and there was added mileage on the odometer. It was obvious that someone had moved and tampered with our car. The next day, I made some calls to stores that used that parking lot to see if there were any security cameras around. One store owner who had been there for many years said that he knew for a fact that there were no cameras because that topic had come up before. I was concerned about the tires because I have read that car tires are a favorite place to hide covert GPS or following devices on a car. I know that our cars have GPS devices on them because the stalkers always know where our cars are.

Another retail stalking/spying incident happened a few days later. Since this began, there have been hundreds (thousands?) of incidents of being followed and stalked in a store, restaurant, airport, hotel, theater, mall, etc. As I have said, I could not possibly document all of them here, and some of them are more obvious than others. It is amazing how unobservant some people must think we are. It usually seems as if they really don't care if we spot them as stalkers or not. They are always extraordinarily interested in what I am buying, my conversations, how much I spend, how I pay for something, etc. It has led me to the conclusion that maybe the stalking participants get points for information like this, or maybe they are told to try to make their targets uncomfortable with their extreme interest and intrusions.

I had taken a print to a frame shop to be framed. The store owner called to tell me it was ready to be picked up, and I said I would stop by on Monday afternoon to pick it up. This frame shop is in a large open mall with several parking areas. As I drove in, there was a man in a black truck parked diagonally across a few parking spots. He was sitting in his truck as if he were looking for someone or something. As soon as I drove by to go park in front of the frame shop, he started his engine, followed me, and pulled into the spot right next to me. Since that seemed a bit odd to me, I decided to stay in my car for a minute and let him go where he needed to go. I started to check my cell phone. He finally got out of his truck and went into the frame shop, so I thought I would just wait for him to come out before I went in. Before I became a stalking victim, I would have never done that. I would never have even assumed that he was following me. Now, I would just as soon skip being looked at and followed, even in a relatively safe setting.

I stayed in my car for another five minutes until he came out and got into his truck. I thought I could go in without having my privacy invaded. No such luck. I walked into the shop, and the owner came out from the back. We chatted for a minute, and she said she would go to the back and get my print. While she was in the back, the man from the black truck came back into the shop! The store owner came out with my print and saw that he was back. She said, "Are there more questions I can answer for you?" I could tell from her tone of voice that she hoped there weren't. He answered, "Yes, but I'll just wait until you're finished." He then stood there watching as I looked at my framed print, conversed with the store owner, paid for it, and she helped me out to put it in the back of my car.

For a period of several months, our main television set that we watch the most would turn off by itself while we were watching it. This happened quite a few times – probably 15 or 20. Sometimes, it would come back on a minute later. It was as if someone outside our house had a compatible remote for our set, and they were playing games with us. I suspect the neighbor behind us, Adam, as their house is close enough that a remote would probably work from there.

I have suspected that my email has been hacked into for many years. Just as with telephone conversations, there have been obvious stalker incidents when everything was arranged by email. It seems to be no more private than our landline or cell phones. What happened in January of 2008 forced me to change email servers after at least ten years with the same email account and address. I had a small but reliable email server for many years. I didn't change because I didn't want to change my longstanding email address. The problem was that as of several months earlier, email customers could no longer change passwords online. It had to be done by telephone, and all it required was giving them your email address and the answer to a "secret question." My question was the name of the city where I was born. That was an easy one for my stalkers. It really wouldn't have mattered since I had to get my new password by phone and I knew my phone was not secure.

Something happened one day in January with the server software, and I could no longer get to their website, let alone my email. Apparently, no one could access their server for a day or so. Around that time, a hacker/stalker must have tried to access my emails for the day and couldn't. I can only guess that he thought I had found a way to change my password. In reality, I hadn't changed it in quite a while. When the server became available, I tried to sign on to my email, and it kept saying that I was entering the incorrect password. I called them to see what might be wrong, and they said they had reset my password when I had called the previous evening. They told me that they log all calls to reset passwords. I told them I had never called and asked if they could tell me what phone number the person had called from. They said they couldn't without a court order, and I would have to file a police report to get a court order. As far as they were concerned, I had called and asked them to reset it. At that point, I asked to have a new password so I could read my mail, and they gave me one. I quickly acted to set up a new email account with another company.

I also decided to file a report with the local police station, but nothing ever came of it. I never heard from them again. That has also been the case on other occasions when I have reported identity theft issues to the local police. They tell you that you need to file a police report if you want to pursue it, but it has not seemed to do any good in my experience.

I planned to meet a friend for lunch one day in January. I was going to pick her up, and we arranged it by phone, including discussing the restaurant where we would go. The night before, we had a snowstorm, and that morning I discussed with Mark whether I should just reschedule lunch for another day. I was strongly considering it when our next-door neighbor Stan, out of the blue, brought his snow blower over and cleared the side of the driveway where my car was. This was surprising for several reasons. This was the first time he had ever done that in the three winters we have lived in this house. Also, I don't go out every single day, so I was puzzled why he suddenly decided to clear my side of the driveway on that particular day, especially because it was a weekday and he had to go to work. Also, he came over to clear it before Mark even left for work. It seemed so farfetched that it made me wonder if he somehow knew that I was contemplating staying home that day because of the snow.

We ended up having an intruder in the house while I was gone that day! I ended up being gone for at least a couple of hours. The stalkers knew when and where I would be going, and I am certain they were watching us, or at least my car in the parking lot. When I returned home, I found several things tampered with. A light bulb had been replaced with an off brand, two brand-new lamps were tampered with, the light bulb sockets were now loose, and a glass cover for a ceiling light fixture (which was 11 feet high) in the master bathroom had been either exchanged or damaged. The white colored glass looked like it had been smeared with something that took the color off of part of it. I ended up having to have it replaced!

Also, I had just put a new ink cartridge in my printer. The next time I used it, it said it was low on ink. I know some printers say that well before you really need to replace them, but this was a brand-new full-size printer ink cartridge. It was as if someone had used the copier (or printer) function for printing a hundred pages.

Since I had recently purchased a printer that would leave no proof of what was printed or copied, they used my equipment and ink to copy whatever they wanted after they illegally entered our home! I can only imagine that this might have included my list of online passwords, medical reports, bank and other financial statements, my calendar, and whatever other documents on my computer or in my file cabinet that they thought they needed. Before this printer/copier, only my traditional fax machine was capable of making copies. I discovered years ago that the stalkers had used it to copy some things because each page copied or faxed showed up on the film cartridge. When I found the film cartridge almost full, I took it out to look at it. I must have talked about it out loud, because I didn't notice it again. It still may have been used, but not for large numbers of documents at a time like the first time. Not enough that I would bother to take the film cartridge out to see what was on it.

After knowing for sure that there had been in-truders in the house while I was gone that day, I began to wonder about our next-door neighbor who made sure I would be able to get out of my driveway that day. It is certainly sad that instead of thinking that he was just being a good neighbor, I entertain the fact that he is also involved with the stalkers. Stan doesn't seem to be the type who would take money to spy on his neighbors. I wondered what in the world they could say to get him to cooperate. It is also possible that this neighbor, as well as others, has accidentally discovered that he can hear everything in our house through some type of receiver or scanner used for entertainment or hobby. In other words, he may have accidentally discovered how to hear the transmissions from our hidden transmitters instead of being told exactly how to receive them by someone. If anyone would do that and not bother to ever tell us, I would say they are as guilty of criminal activity as the organized stalkers are!

I could only think of three possibilities. First, just by sheer chance, Stan decided to clear my half of our driveway for the first and only time in 3 years on a day when we ended up with intruders in the house. Second, he had accidentally found the frequency where our voices transmit and he heard me say I was considering canceling my plans for the day. He was trying to be a good neighbor by clearing our driveway so I could get out more easily. Third, perhaps he is involved with the stalkers in some way, and he was asked to make sure my side of the driveway was cleared so I would leave the house and they could enter as planned. The stalkers knew that I had an appointment to have a new security system installed in a few weeks, so it was probably important to them that they get into the house that day.

I had the new security/surveillance system installed, and soon after that, I had the locks changed again. This time, I thought I took extra precautions to make sure no "extra" keys could be made by the locksmith. That was one of the explanations I had for how they could keep entering without obvious signs of forced entry. My research showed that no matter what they say, most locksmiths can be bribed to make an extra key. I will say that I'm sure they have standards. The person doing the bribing would have to have a very good story (lie) and be quite persuasive to get the locksmith's cooperation, or the bribe would have to be substantial enough and have a good story to go along with it. Within two months, they were back in.

Over the years, there has been a very loud noise that seemed to come from inside whatever portable television we have had in our bedroom. I never heard this noise before 1994, and even though I have heard it dozens of times, Mark has never been in the room when it happens. It is most common when he is out of town, but it has also happened when he is in another part of the house watching television, where he sometimes falls asleep. The noise sounds like an extremely loud bang, almost like a gun, and it usually occurs just as I have fallen asleep. It is loud enough to wake me up from a deep sleep, and it does.

I don't know what kind of device could do this, but I have to assume that someone triggers the sound with a remote device. I would guess that it's someone in a neighboring house or a nearby car. This has happened with two different televisions and in every house we've lived. It is not only extremely disturbing to be awakened like that; it confirms to me that they are watching our every move, whether by cameras or some other equipment. We bought a smaller, flat panel set not too long ago, and it was so nice to know it might not happen again, but we are still getting some very loud noises. Mark was out of town the last time it happened – at 1:30 a.m. I woke up to the extremely loud sound, but I couldn't tell for sure if it came from the television, the windows, or even my exercise bike. Before the stalking began, I never in my life heard sounds like these, but now it happens frequently.

The catchcanada.org website (see Appendix One) lists "Banging and tapping of walls, windows and objects in the house" as just one of many types of harassment technology used by organized stalking groups. I came across that information only a couple of years ago, and it certainly describes what could be happening in our house.

I knew that the intrusions were still going on, but I still have no explanation for how an intruder could be in the house at night when the locks and inside bolts are set. As I mentioned earlier, the only things I can think of are that one or more people are hiding in the attic or crawlspace areas, or that there is some obscure way of entering the house that we are unaware of. Although this might not sound probable or feasible, I have to consider the possibilities.

Several weeks ago, Mark was out of town on business and Cindy was away at college. I was home alone. Recently, that seems to be the optimal time for intrusion and/or harassment activities. Actually, it always has been, but over the years, there have been periods of time when Mark didn't do much work-related travel. When I woke up in the morning, I felt like I had been in a deep sleep all night. It is difficult to describe why I thought I felt like that, but I have felt it before. However, since I was asleep and didn't wake up all night, I really had no explanation. That morning, I saw that the vanity stool in our bathroom had been moved. I keep it in a certain place so I won't trip over it, and it had been moved out toward the middle of the room. Also, a piece of hidden surveillance equipment that I had turned on the night before had been tampered with and turned off. I checked the doors, and they were all still locked and bolted from the inside. That was all I had to go on. What had happened that night?

Almost on a daily basis, I continue to have all of the many types of harassment tactics used on me. Vehicles will pull out of parking lots and follow me for long distances, seeming to stay behind me if possible. We continue to have home intrusions, our property and belongings tampered with, all our phones tapped, mail tampered with, email hacked into, strange things happening with appliances, loud noises in the middle of the night, people sitting in their cars when I come out from any store or appointment, and on and on. I have had several instances where I will get a call that seems like a wrong number, and I will ask what number they were trying to call. They have given my number on several occasions, and they have said the person put it down on an application, or left the number on a message, or even that they received a pager call with my number on it.

As I am working on this book, strange things continue to happen. Something similar to what happened to my email server password recently happened to the password on a savings account. I went to log on, and it said the password I had entered was incorrect. Neither Mark nor I had changed the password in a while, but someone had. Apparently, one of the stalkers wanted to access the account and didn't have our latest password. He had the account information and the answers to the secret questions, and he (she?) was able to reset the password online. Either the firm doesn't send out email alerts when a password is changed or the stalker intercepted the email because we were never notified.

There have been many other situations like this. I wrote about the telephone access to our bank accounts many years before, but there have been several password changes since we started accessing more information by computer. On financial accounts, we are more likely to change passwords more frequently. I'm quite sure that each time they break in to our house they get an updated copy of my list of passwords. The stalkers seem to have a problem if they can't access one of our accounts when they want to. They have changed other passwords by simply answering a few questions. They seem to have made it their business to know as much personal data on us as they can.

Within a few weeks of having one of our financial accounts hacked into, someone completely took over one of our credit cards. I received an email notification that our account information had been updated as requested. It said to notify them immediately if I did not make this request. When I notified them, everything on the account had been changed except our names, which cannot be changed.

I asked them for the new account information, and they gave it to me. That was after I answered a few personal identifying questions, which obviously someone else was able to answer. I called the phone number they had listed, and it was a fax machine. I know many people have their credit card numbers stolen, but this was more than that. The thief changed all of our account information online, and he had to have Mark's mother's maiden name and the last four digits of Mark's social security number to make the changes.

What I will never understand is being that obsessed with the minute details of other peoples' lives.

I have read that if the organized stalking goes on long enough, the people involved (the perpetrators) will change every so often. This seems probable when there is an out-of-state move, but it also happens if the target stays in the same city. The leaders of the group may change or stay the same. As the years have gone by, I have noticed that some of the tactics remain the same, but others change. Some are almost eliminated for a while, and other new ones are added.

CHAPTER NINE

SERVICE PEOPLE

There has been much written about how service people are often approached, bribed and manipulated by organized stalking groups. The purpose is to enlist their help in victimizing the targets. I have strongly suspected that this has happened to me on several occasions. The usual pattern is much the same as what has been documented by others. Several times, I have had an initial meeting with a person I have hired or invited to my home to give me an estimate on some work. Everything has gone well, and they get started on the job. Suddenly, they turn into a different person, there are long delays, or they seem to purposely do a bad job.

I found this hard to figure out for a long time, and then I realized that these people had to have been bribed, and probably for more than what they were going to charge for the whole job. Why else would they chance hurting their reputations or potentially not even getting paid? No one but the stalkers knows what lies they tell to get their cooperation.

The most extreme example involved a security company salesperson, Ron, who was supposed to arrange for the replacement of some surveillance system equipment in 2007. I had talked to him several times, in person and over the phone, and I considered him to be professional and trustworthy. However, he ended up being fired from his job for what he did. I thought I knew him well enough that I never suspected anything until the whole scam was almost over. He was not working alone, and whatever they offered him must have made it worthwhile!

Basically, he made extensive misrepresentations and told numerous lies about replacing the equipment. Over a period of five months, thirty-three appointments were scheduled and then cancelled, almost always on the day of the appointment. Many times, Ron showed up at our door at the appointed time and gave me another excuse. Sometimes he cancelled by phone. The excuses were usually about problems they had suddenly found with similar equipment, installers who were sick that day, or potential weather problems. He also claimed several times that there were problems with a computer chip in the equipment, or that they needed to do more testing to make sure the equipment would work.

He appeared to be the most serious and apologetic individual I had ever met. It turned out that he was a scam artist. Nothing he said turned out to be true. In hindsight, I believe this was all done to inconvenience and frustrate me so that my reactions could be documented, or perhaps they continued rewarding Ron for as long as he could keep the game going. Either way, something was going on.

About halfway through all of this, he made an offer to me that was probably an attempt to keep me involved. He said that they were going to exchange the equipment AND refund all of what I had paid for it to make up for all of the incredible inconvenience they had caused. He said his boss had authorized this, and they felt it was the right thing to do. He said that they would be using a brand of equipment they had not used before, and I would be a test site for it. That was the reason he gave for refunding the money. However, he never refunded anything, and there was never any new equipment. It was all part of the scam.

Eventually, I still became frustrated by how long it was taking, so he added to the incentive. He then told me that they were going to refund all money paid, provide new equipment so that I could be a test site, AND they were going to add an additional $500.00 since I had been so cooperative. Of course it sounded too good to be true, but Ron was always completely serious and persuasive. He assured me that all of this was going to happen. It never did.

He continued to tell me that he was working with his boss to resolve the problems, but it turned out that his boss knew nothing about what he was doing. Ron provided incredible detail in everything he said. He gave names and details about people that I didn't think anyone would go to the trouble to fabricate. I finally became so suspicious that I told him I was beginning to question his stories and wondered if this was some sort of scam. I still believed his boss knew everything he had done, so I threatened to call the police and report him and his company if it was a scam. He got very upset, almost angry, and denied anything of the sort.

The next day, he called to apologize. He sounded frantic and on the verge of some kind of breakdown. He now told a whole new story. He confessed that his boss knew nothing of what he had been doing. He kept saying that he had been so stupid, and he never meant to hurt anyone. He said he had "hurt so many people." He also said that he got involved with people that he never should have. He asked me not to call the police and said he had a wife and three children to support. He again apologized for everything he had done as far as the misrepresentations and lies. He blamed the "people he got involved with," whom he claimed he had met in a bar. He would go into no more detail, and that was the last time I ever spoke with him.

I called his boss, Bob, that day and related the whole story to him. He could barely respond because he was so shocked. He said he knew nothing about it, and he didn't know that Ron could be capable of doing such a thing. I gave him some of the names and companies that Ron had mentioned over the months, and he said he had never heard of them. I told him that my main concern was finding out who Ron was referring to when he said he "got involved with these people." Of course, Bob's main concern was what to do with Ron and how to make sure he hadn't involved any of his other customers. He said that there was nothing that should have kept Ron from replacing the equipment months earlier. He offered to send someone else out right away to do so, but I had lost all confidence by that time.

I spoke to Bob a few more times after that. Ron had been immediately terminated from his job when he would give no explanation for what he had done. It appears he preferred to be fired than reveal what and with whom he had gotten involved. Bob made Ron promise that he would seek ongoing mental health therapy. I went elsewhere for our equipment needs. Bob still believes that Ron had just decided to live in a fantasy world of lies. I'm not so sure.

Several months ago, I discovered that the driver for a package delivery service was opening many of my packages. I have had packages delivered by this company for many years, and I have never had any problems until this driver started delivering. He has delivered many of my packages with the tape completely undone. It is usually pressed back on, but it is obvious that it was removed so that the box could be completely opened and the contents revealed. I confronted the driver about it, and his response was that he has to deliver them if they are loaded on his truck that way. He said that was the way they were all loaded on his truck. Before I confronted him, he often pulled up to the front of our house and stayed in his truck for at least five minutes before bringing the package(s) to the front porch.

I assume there is a possibility that he was already a member of the organized stalking game when he started on this route. It's also possible that one of them could have reached out to him and convinced him to report details on all deliveries to our house. I sometimes forget that as hard as I try, I am never going to understand how their organization works or what their motivation is. I am never going to understand the mind of a sociopathic stalker. The point is that for several months, for whatever reason, this particular driver seemed to have an unusual interest in deliveries to our house. One time, he delivered a package that needed a signature. It had the package tape completely removed, but the item inside the box had been extremely well wrapped and taped with tissue paper. It was impossible to know what it was. He was so curious about what it was that he actually asked me. I just replied that it was something I had ordered. None of these incidents have ever really looked like package damage in transit. They looked more like intentional tampering to see the contents of the package.

CHAPTER TEN

FINAL THOUGHTS AND CONCLUSIONS

Writing this book has enlightened me in some ways. Even though I don't have the answers for what has been and is happening, writing about these incidents has made me even more aware of what disturbed and dangerous people are involved in organized stalking.

Something else that writing this book has made me see is that more often than not, the stalkers want their targets to know that they are being stalked. For many years, I thought that they were trying to be covert or discreet. As I wrote about the incidents I included in this book, I realized more and more that very few of them have ever tried to be covert – just the opposite. As most of the documentation on organized stalking states, they want their targets to know they are being followed, watched, etc.

Although I had no idea what was happening, it seemed to take my mind several years to allow for the idea that someone was trying to physically and mentally hurt me and my family. It just wasn't part of my mindset to think about the purposeful evil deeds of others. I now feel nothing but contempt for my stalkers. Writing this book has not been a labor of love. In fact, being forced to relive and review everything has been extremely difficult. I kept at it because I believe it is a subject that has to be exposed.

As a victim, I have tried many times to put what is happening out of my mind, even for brief periods of time, yet it has never stopped for any period of time. They do not want their targets to have any peace, even while sleeping. Organized stalking is not only a hate crime; it is a form of abuse. I don't think any normal person would argue with the fact that a large, organized group stalking someone around the clock is abusive behavior.

I have so many unanswered questions. I have asked myself for so long why these creeps have continued to stalk me and my family. Our lives are just ordinary. Since we are not whistleblowers, political activists or celebrities, why not go after someone else?

I can only speculate. Maybe it is a matter of becoming obsessed in some way with a target family, no matter how ordinary their lives are. This is not the type of obsession one usually hears about. This is what I would call "victim obsession." They have invested so much time and effort to learn the details of our lives that they are not going to leave us alone. The thrill is in continuing the game. The times we have moved to a new city in a new state, they have had to start all over again. Why bother? Why us? Why not just start stalking the people who moved into our house?

I wonder how their conversations go when we change our locks or get a new car or plan an out-of-town trip. Do they start talking by phone or text message, or is everything arranged over the Internet? How many of them get involved in each decision? How is the "work" assigned? What kind of work ethic do sociopathic organized stalkers have?

One of the questions targets of organized stalk-ing are asked is why they think they are so special or interesting that anyone would want to stalk them. The answer is that we're not! There are all sorts of reasons people are selected as targets, and some of the reasons are random. This is a hate crime, and the target may never know what or who is behind it.

Something about which I feel strongly enough to speak out against is any kind of injustice against people. This includes any type of mistreatment or abuse of others. Obviously, that describes the very purpose of organized stalking groups. These groups mistreat and abuse the rights of their targets. How ironic that they convince themselves that they are somehow performing a service!

I always assumed that if the stalking activities against me were ever revealed to a friend, relative, or even an acquaintance, they would tell me immediately. Then I began to wonder if I should be so sure. If a stalker is so twisted, tells such twisted lies, and does such twisted things, maybe they wouldn't tell me. The literature on organized stalking says the stalkers will use recorded conversations to turn others against the target. If they identify a need, they will impersonate the victim on the phone or in a recording. Whatever it takes to mess with the targets' lives is within the scope of their purpose.

How many people have never said something negative about another person on the phone or in the privacy of their home? It happens. What if the next time you said something – anything – negative about someone, a recording of what you said was played for that person? How might that affect your relationship? That is how they operate. Just to give one example, suppose that I said something to a friend on the phone, or to my husband, that I didn't like the way my hair stylist had been doing my hair lately and I was considering changing stylists. The next time I go back to her, she is curt and cold toward me, even though she never acted that way before. Things like that have happened to me numerous times since this started. Often, I have never said anything negative, but a stalker intervenes after I have had an initial encounter with someone. The next time I meet them, they act differently – as if they have been told something horrible about me.

Playing games like this make the stalkers feel powerful and in control. This is what they live for. As I said, many of the people in a stalking group don't even know why they don't like the targets. It is just assumed that they deserve to be stalked and harassed at all times. I think it would be normal for someone hearing about organized stalking for the first time to wonder if one of us had done something quite horrible to deserve this sort of harassment. I can assure you that we have not. I believe we were selected randomly, or one of us was in the wrong place at the wrong time. Some targets are selected for a specific reason or cause, but nothing justifies treating people this way.

I also believe the leader of the group stalking me has used the organized stalking participants to get help in keeping tabs on me at all times. He couldn't do that alone. He uses lies, bribes, promises, or whatever it takes to convince people to do what he wants. How would he have even known how to contact such a group? Even today, how many people know such groups exist, or how to approach them? I only know about them because I have been their victim. How do people who use them to victimize others know about them? How do people know about this very dark side of life? There are some experts in the field of organized stalking who suggest that the names of targets are submitted to the "torturers." Since I don't know why or how I was selected, I do believe this is possible.

There was an incident that happened just months after the stalking began that I will mention at this time. It was so bizarre and yet so personal that I was going to omit it, but I think it adds to all the anecdotal evidence presented. In 1994, I went to the gynecologist for a Pap test and exam. I had gone to this doctor for a few years. His female assistant was in the exam room also. Before he started the exam, he said to his assistant, in a rather low voice, that he would need two samples – one to send to the lab, and one for "him," referring to someone else. He then rolled his eyes. I had absolutely no idea what he was talking about, or even if he was actually talking about me. However, he did take two swabs at that time, and I had never had that happen before.

Again, I don't know why I didn't speak up at the time, but later that day, I thought of a few questions I should have asked! The bigger question is to whom was he referring? Who needed his own sample of my cells? It had to have been a very convincing individual to persuade a doctor to do that. It seems like it would have to have been someone else in the medical field, but even then, what kind of reason could he or she give?

I have gone back after the fact to follow up on strange incidents or comments, and it has never done any good. I have usually been answered with double talk. The time for me to ask would have been at the moment he said it in front of his assistant. Even then, he could have told me that he was talking about someone else, or any number of other replies. The point is that I know he took two samples from me that day, and someone had requested that second slide. How odd!

Every time I leave my house, I wonder if someone will try to enter while I am gone. I leave the house knowing that someone, somewhere, is aware that I am leaving, and any number of people will soon know that I am driving somewhere. Every time I use one of our phones, I wonder who might be listening and how many people will eventually be able to listen to my phone conversation. Every time I have a conversation inside our house, I wonder who will hear it, and maybe even who will see it. Every time I take a shower, I wonder about a hidden camera. Every time I have a conversation inside our car, I wonder which people in nearby cars are secretly listening. Every email sent and received is potentially shared. Everything I order online is probably documented for these creeps. It is all part of their invasive, obsessive game.

Every single day, I fear for the lives, health and safety of my husband, my daughter and myself. I continue to fear what the stalkers are doing to our home and our belongings every single time they enter our home. I continue to wonder how and why they operate and why they selected us as targets. I continue to believe that this is more than just a game – they are dangerous and need to be exposed.

I need to be able to focus on my life, my health and my happiness. I need to be able to go out without worrying that sick sociopathic stalkers are waiting to enter my home when I leave or follow me wherever I go. I need to know I can live the rest of my life without constantly worrying about why this is happening.

I no longer feel envy of any kind except for the envy I feel for all the people who live peaceful and private lives. I have no envy of other peoples' homes, families, careers, looks, good health or possessions. I have no envy of anything other people have except the peace and privacy other people enjoy. It is funny that peace and privacy are things we take for granted; they are not fully appreciated until they are taken away from us.

I will end this book by saying that I promise you this is a true story. I couldn't have made it up if I had tried – I just don't have that kind of imagination. All of these events really happened as I have reported them. One thing that understandably happens after so many years of being stalked is that a target may suspect an innocent person or an uninvolved car as being part of the stalker group. Most targets will readily admit that some things just happen to everyone, and sometimes they are wrong about suspecting a certain individual who, it turns out, is not involved. That does not negate the fact that the ongoing stalking activities really happen. I feel a great motivation to move ahead in the process of trying to expose what has happened to me and to help expose the concept of organized stalking.

Life is full of choices. I never chose nor even imagined that I could become a victim of such an evil, heinous crime as organized stalking. However, perhaps I chose to allow it to go on for this long because of denial and ignorance about what was happening. The stalkers all make a very conscious choice every day to continue to participate in this crime. I believe they will all pay a price for it someday.

I think that all victims of organized stalking should be able to file civil and/or criminal charges against their perpetrators. Why are the perps allowed to break into their victims' cars and homes and have no consequences? The FBI says that they don't handle stalking cases, and the local law enforcement doesn't often help, either.

We need to be more vocal about this crime. To do this, we need more proof. We need more details. We need to appeal for information from some of those who are or were involved as members of a stalking group. It may get worse before it gets better; some say that trying to expose them will just make them more active and aggressive. However, I agree with those who say that if we want to stop it, we need to expose organized stalking and the people involved. It is a crime from which we have very little protection. It is often impossible to prove, and it really can happen to anyone.

APPENDIXES

Appendix One   Websites on Organized Stalking

Appendix Two   Organized Stalking Brochure
                    Published as part of the infor-
                    mation package offered on the
                    catchcanada.org website.

Appendix Three   Organized Stalking FAQ
                    Published as part of the infor-
                    mation package offered on the
                    catchcanada.org website. Sum-
                    marized from *Terrorist Stalking
                    in America* by David Lawson.

Appendix Four   Quotes from David Lawson's
                    Terrorist Stalking in America.
                    Published as part of the infor-
                    mation package offered on the
                    catchcanada.org website.

All materials in the appendices are reprinted with
permission.

APPENDIX ONE

WEBSITES ON ORGANIZED STALKING AND TECHNOLOGICAL HARASSMENT

www.catchcanada.org, temporarily available at www.multistalkervictims.org/catchcanada

www.freedomfchs.com

www.gangstalking.ca

www.gangstalkingworld.com

www.multistalkervictims.org

www.psychologicalharassment.com

www.stopcovertwar.com

Sources for this book included some of the websites listed above.

APPENDIX TWO

Introduction

Citizens Against Technological and Community-Based Harassment ("CATCH") is a Canadian-based activism and support group dedicated to helping victims of a virtually unknown form of criminal activity.

We work in conjunction with our local Rape Crisis Centre.

Our activism efforts are directed towards raising public awareness as well as educating those in the helping professions.

CATCH deals with two types of criminal activity: "technological harassment" and "community-based harassment". The majority of victims experience both. However, this information package focuses specifically on community-based harassment.

By taking the time to better understand this crime, you will not only help us to be heard, but you will be able to provide victims who contact you with a much-needed source of support and validation.

Thank you for taking the time to read our information package.

Definition

Community-based Harassment:

❖ Community-based harassment is a form of "criminal harassment", which is defined by the Canadian Department of Justice[2] as follows:

> Criminal harassment, which includes 'stalking', is a crime. While many crimes are defined by conduct that results in a very clear outcome (for example, murder), criminal harassment generally consists of repeated conduct that is carried out over a period of time and that causes victims to reasonably fear for their safety, but does not necessarily result in physical injury.

❖ As opposed to a 'conventional' stalking situation, which involves a single stalker, this activity involves the use of *multiple individuals* to:
  o Stalk a victim
  o Harass a victim (usually indirectly),
  o Vandalize personal property,
  o Enter a person's house when they are away, and
  o Sometimes attempt to discredit a victim at work and in the community.

❖ It is an ongoing and concerted effort to destroy an individual's life, which is very often successful.

❖ Because multiple stalkers are involved, the stalking can take place *every* time the victim leaves his or her home.

❖ Noise campaigns are common.

❖ Incidents are intentionally repetitive so that they stand out from normal random incidents. This process is known as "sensitizing the target[1]" to the presence of the perpetrators.

❖ Community-based harassment is also referred to as:
  o organized stalking
  o group stalking
  o gang stalking
  o cause-stalking[1]
  o vengeance stalking[1]
  o vigilante-style stalking[1], and
  o stalking-by-proxy[3]

❖ This is a form of *psychological warfare*, intended to break down the target's defenses, but is also a way for perpetrators who feel powerless to empower themselves.

Definition - 2

The U.S. Department of Justice website defines "Vengeance/ Terrorism Stalking"[4] as follows:

The final stalking category is fundamentally different from the other three. Vengeance stalkers do not seek a personal relationship with their targets. Rather, vengeance/terrorist stalkers attempt to elicit a particular response or a change of behavior from their victims. When vengeance is their prime motive, stalkers seek only to punish their victims for some wrong they perceive the victim has visited upon them. In other words, they use stalking as a means to "get even" with their enemies.

The most common scenario in this category involves employees who stalk employers after being fired from their job. Invariably, the employee believes that their dismissal was unjustified and that their employer or supervisor was responsible for unjust treatment. One bizarre variation on this pattern is the case of a scout master who was dismissed for inappropriate conduct and subsequently decided to stalk his entire former scout troop - scouts and scout leaders alike.

A second type of vengeance or terrorist stalker, the political stalker, has motivations that parallel those of more traditional terrorists. That is, stalking is a weapon of terror used to accomplish a political agenda. Utilizing the threat of violence to force the stalking target to engage in or refrain from engaging in particular activity. For example, most prosecutions in this stalking category have been against anti-abortionists who stalk doctors in an attempt to discourage the performance of abortions.

"Cyber-stalking":

The majority of victims of community-based harassment also feel that their online activites are monitored. In addition, they encounter frequent issues with 'lost' emails as well as ongoing virus-like behavior on their computers, despite taking extensive precautions to prevent these intrusions.

See FAQ and Appendix 1 for more information.

Effects on Victims

Because community-based harassment may go on for many years, the psychological and health effects on the victims can be severe.

Psychological effects include:

- ❖ Severe depression with a strong tendency towards thoughts of suicide
- ❖ Destruction of self-esteem
- ❖ Loss of faith
- ❖ Loss of purpose
- ❖ Progressive social isolation
- ❖ Ongoing post-traumatic stress disorder

Other effects include:

- ❖ Destruction of personal relationships
- ❖ Loss of livelihood
- ❖ Loss of possessions due to cessation of income
- ❖ Financial strain due to constant repairs of cars and other vandalized items
- ❖ Loss of respect of friends and family
- ❖ The development of mental health issues *as a result* of the stress
- ❖ Labeling - "paranoid", "mentally ill", "schizophrenic"

From the Canadian Department of Justice report on criminal harassment entitled, "Harassment: A Handbook for Police and Crown Prosecutors"[2], some common responses by victims to the trauma of being stalked include:

- ❖ Self reproach
- ❖ A tendency to downplay the impact of the stalking
- ❖ Interpretation of the stalking as a 'private matter'
- ❖ A sense of betrayal and stigma
- ❖ Anxiety and fear due to the unpredictability of the stalker's conduct
- ❖ Feelings of being helpless and unable to control their lives
- ❖ Lack of confidence in the Police, resulting in a *failure to report*
- ❖ Inaction, due to a lack of awareness that the conduct is criminal
- ❖ Denial or embarrassment.

The Issue of Mental Illness

It goes without saying that there are parallels between this situation and genuine cases of "paranoid delusion", which can make it hard for helping professionals, non-victims (and fellow victims alike) to establish the truth of a particular individual's case.

However, when the situation is taken as a whole, rather than as a series *single, isolated* events, the picture which is formed is strikingly consistent between targets. Without taking the time to hear a victim's story, as well as to look beyond the panic and anguish that usually accompanies the early stages of the harassment, the difference between this situation and a delusional state of mind may not be *initially* evident.

When seeing a helping professional, many victims often experience what is known as the "Martha Mitchell Effect"[5]:

> Sometimes improbable reports are erroneously assumed to be symptoms of mental illness (Maher, 1988). The 'Martha Mitchell effect' referred to the tendency of mental health practitioners to not believe the experience of the wife of the American attorney general, whose persistent reports of corruption in the Nixon White House were initially dismissed as evidence of delusional thinking, until later proved correct by the Watergate investigation.

> Such examples demonstrate that delusional pathology can often lie in the failure or inability to verify whether the events have actually taken place, no matter how improbable intuitively they might appear to the busy clinician. Clearly there are instances 'where people are pursued by the Mafia' or are 'kept under surveillance by the police', and where they rightly suspect 'that their spouse is unfaithful' (Sedler, 1995). As Joseph H. Berke (1998) wrote, even paranoids have enemies! For understandable and obvious reasons, however, little effort is invested by the clinicians into checking the validity of claims of persecution or harassment, and without such evidence the patient could be labeled delusional.

This is the uphill battle which victims of organized stalking and harassment are facing: *Is it possible to reach out for help without being re-victimized by those in the helping professions?* The damage caused by the stalking can be so great that a victim may choose to never report it.

"Why You?"

One of the most common questions asked of the victims is "Why you?" In many cases, victims don't know why they've been targeted, and as a result are rarely believed by friends and family due to the subtle and subjective nature of the harassment. It is extremely difficult for victims to gather solid evidence.

The activity of the stalking groups is very similar to that of other hate/extremist groups. According to David Lawson, who wrote *Terrorist Stalking in America*[1], these methods of harassment have been modeled on those developed by the Ku Klux Klan and refined over decades. Lawson refers to these groups as "cults", in which the interaction between members is more important than the interaction with the targets. (See Appendix 1).

In addition, Lawson states that "the primary targets of all these tactics are *the group members*, not the target. The group members are the ones who are programmed. Group leaders define reality for their members... Stalking various targets is only part of the activity of these groups. Members are trained to perform a variety of activities *without question*. They do not know the objectives of their leaders... [However], those targeted for harassment will have no problem concluding that someone is after them, but *most never know who it is*."(pp. 42,43,51) (*Note: Lawson refers to the stalkers as "group members".*)

If we don't know who is doing it, it is difficult to guess why it's being done. However, most people can understand revenge as a possible motive for stalking or harassment. If you go online and do a search on the word "revenge" you may be shocked at what you see. Revenge has not only become an acceptable part of the sub-culture, those who promote it refer to themselves as "revengists" or "avengers". People are targeted when they deserve to be "taught a lesson". But the lessons are invariably cruel, and the perpetrators revel in keeping their identities a secret. This activity is empowering for the perpetrators, so they continue to do it.

It's important to note that the stalkers themselves are not the ones who have initiated the harassment, but are being used (i.e. "stalkers by proxy"[3]) by an unknown individual (or corporation) to carry out the harassment. The stalkers do not know the victims personally.

Many victims have referred to their experiences as "rape", and the emotional dynamics between perpetrators and victim in both situations may be very similar.

142

Statistics

CATCH estimates that as many as 1 in 100 people (1%) may be victims of organized stalking at some point in their lives.

Stalking Studies:

American Journal of Psychiatry:
❖ In 6/201 cases (approx. 3%) respondents reported multiple stalkers[22].

Howard Journal of Criminal Justice[23]:
❖ In 5/95 cases (approx. 5%) perpetrators were part of a group
❖ 40% of victims (38) said that friends and or family of their stalker had also been involved in their harassment (stalking-by-proxy)
❖ All cases of multiple stalkers involved mixed sex stalker groups
❖ In 15% of cases, the victim could provide no possible reason for their harassment
❖ 13% reported that their homes had been bugged
❖ 32% reported that the stalker(s) broke into/damaged the inside of the victim's home
❖ 38% reported damage to the outside of the home
❖ 30% reported that the stalker(s) stole from the victim,
❖ 91% reported being watched
❖ 82% reported being followed
❖ 60% reported having their character slandered/defamed
❖ 84% were victim to repetitive phone calls
❖ 60% reported hang up phone calls
❖ 57% reported silent calls
❖ 46% reported negative attitude from the police, and 51% reported negative actions

British Home Office[7]:
❖ It is estimated that about 1,900,000 people (ages 16-59) in England and Wales were victims of stalking in the year 2000. That is about 3.6%, based on a population of 52 million.

Workplace Harassment (or "Mobbing"):

❖ It is estimated that 3.5% of the working population of Sweden is subject to mobbing[6].

Criminal Harassment (Canadian Dept. of Justice):

❖ Although victims always suffered emotional harm, physical injury was recorded by the police in less than 2% of all cases[2].

CATCH Information

Contact information

❖ Email: admin@CatchCanada.org

Website

❖ The following refer to the same website:
www.CatchCanada.org
www.c-a-t-c-h.ca

References

1. Lawson, David. *Terrorist Stalking in America*. Scrambling News. Miami, FL, 2001.

2. http://www.justice.gc.ca/en/ps/fm/pub/harassment/part1.html. Department of Justice, Canada, website. Online version of: "Criminal Harassment: A Handbook for Police and Crown Prosecutors".

3. Mullen, Paul E., Michele Pathe, and Rosemary Purcell. *Stalkers and their Victims*. Cambridge University Press, New York, NY. 2000. pp.173-186.

4. Taken from Chapter 22 in the 1999 *National Victim Assistance Academy Text*. The complete volume is available at the U.S. Department of Justice website (www.usdoj.gov): http://www.ojp.gov/ovc/assist/nvaa99/chap21-2.htm.

5. Bell, Vaughan et. al. "Beliefs About Delusions". *The Psychologist*. Vol. 6 No. 8. August, 2003.

6. Davenport, Dr. Noa et.al. *Mobbing: Emotional Abuse in the American Workplace*. Civil Society Publishing. Ames, Iowa, 1999.

7. http://www.homeoffice.gov.uk/rds/pdfs04/hors276.pdf

8. http://www.netrover.com/~pcawa/stats.html

9. Kamphuis & Emmelkamp. "Traumatic Distress Among Support-Seeking Female Victims of Stalking". *American Journal of Psychiatry*. 158:795-798, May 2001.

10. Sheridan, Davies & Boon. "The Course and Nature of Stalking: A Victim Perspective". *Howard Journal of Criminal Justice*. Volume 40, Number 3, pp. 215-234(20), August 2001.

APPENDIX THREE

Organized Stalking by Groups - FAQ

The following points have been summarized from:
Terrorist Stalking in America
by David Arthur Lawson
Copyright © Scrambling News 2001

David Lawson is a licensed private investigator in Florida (CC2400733). He followed these stalking groups, on and off, for 12 years. He also rode with them. In a recent email, regarding **Canadian stalking groups**, David Lawson said the following:

"When I rode with the group in Niagara Falls/Buffalo, we would seamlessly hook up with Canadians when we crossed the border, and they would ride with us stateside, occasionally."

This gives an indication of just how extensive and well-organized these stalking groups are.

1. Who is behind the stalking groups?
    I. Corporations:
        Groups are used by corporations use to stalk their enemies or potential enemies. (19)
    II. Organized crime:
        Many groups have links to convicted criminals, and associations with organized crime. (24)

2. Who is considered a threat to a corporation or industry?
- Whistleblowers (19)
- Activists (19)

3. What are these groups? (47)
    a. They are private armies.
    b. They are primarily criminal groups.
    c. They have their own targets which are connected to their political agenda.
    d. They are also available for hire, to corporations and other entities, to destroy or neutralize people.
    e. They have the power to destroy lives.

4. How are the groups financed?
- Groups are well financed by: (7)
    i. Corporations (19)
    ii. Other criminal groups (35)
    iii. Committing crimes such as: robbery, theft and drug trafficking (24)
    iv. Some targets are a source of corporate revenue (24)
- Groups are operated as businesses (47)
- The sole financial beneficiaries are the leaders (35)

5. Who are the leaders?
- Leaders pretend that they are larger than life characters, with heroic backgrounds.
- They are looked upon with reverence by their followers.
- Typically, their backgrounds and alleged heroism cannot be independently verified, because it allegedly involves national security.
- Leaders pretend that their groups are committed to bringing about some change.
- In general, group leaders remain isolated from the activities of their followers. (16)
- Leaders do not meet privately with group members. (16)

6. What do the group leaders get out of it?
- Financial power and/or
- Political power

7. Who are the members?

- Right-wing extremist groups (eg. World Church of the Creator (WCOTC) and the Aryan Nations) (9)
- Left-wing extremist groups (9)
- Special interest extremists: (11)
  - animal rights
  - pro-life
  - environmental
  - anti-nuclear
- Because their individual membership is quite small, extremist groups tend to network locally. <u>They're made up of a combination of some people from many different groups in an area.</u> (9)
- Groups cloak their true identities by posing as: (23)
  - citizens groups
  - clubs
  - churches

8. What do the group members get out of it? (15)

- They believe they are fulfilling the 'higher purpose' of the group, even though they may only have a general idea of the ideology of the group.
- They are having fun with their friends, and that fun involves stalking and harassing various targets and engaging in other civil disobedience.
- The people who are attracted to groups which engage in cause stalking are those who feel *powerless*, *inferior* and *angry*. They are empowered by the group.

9. What is the psychology behind all this?

- **This is a game**: (36-37)
  - Groups are rallied by the constant "victories" they win in the games they play with their targets.
  - It does not matter to the group that the targets are not playing a game.
  - It does not matter whether the target even knows what is going on around him.
  - It is most important that *other group members* know what they are doing.
- **This is their entertainment** (45)
- **This is an addiction:** (15)
  - Many become addicted to it.
  - It fulfills some of their human needs (see above).
- **This is an obsession**:
  - Groups are obsessed with every aspect of their target's lives. (37)
  - They spend considerable time describing to one another, what they did, and the target's reaction, although it may not be true. (43)
- **These groups are *cults*:** (37)
  - Groups are introverted - their interaction with one another is more important than their interaction with a target. (36)

10. Who do groups target? (18-19)

- **Public officials** (including local politicians and bureaucrats), IRS agents, Treasury agents.
- **Activists** of all kinds, but especially civil rights activists.
- **Whistleblowers**
- **Abortion workers**
- Identity or white supremacist groups target:
  - **Gays**
  - **African Americans** and
  - **Jewish** people
- Public officials, including Police officers, who have been accused of **wrongdoing**

- Those in the **media**, including radio, television and publishing, especially those who are Jewish and those with fame, but not enough money to isolate themselves from these groups.
- **Immigrants**
- Groups typically target any **judge** presiding over the trial of one of their members.
- Groups also attack **targets of convenience**. These people are selected because they are convenient targets, and not for any other reason. These include loners who tend to be more vulnerable to their harassment tactics than those with family and friends around them. Targets of convenience are used to for practice.
- **Sexual predators**, whose names, addresses and photos are public information which is available on government websites.
- In small towns, where extremist groups can actually have some power, they also target **new people in town** who don't know anyone. The attitude of the extremists is that they control their areas and unknown people can't be trusted.
- Animal rights activists stalk those who own fur ranches, furriers, research scientists working in the field of biomedical research using animals, executives of McDonalds, etc.
- Eco-terrorists target politicians, loggers, etc.
- Groups normally also attack the **family, friends**, and **associates of a target** and even the businesses he patronizes.

11. What purpose does the target serve to the group? (24)
- All targets are important in terms of:
  - rallying groups (i.e. "winning" the game),
  - providing activities,
  - recruiting new members,
  - keeping existing members in line (by example),
  - making a statement to the community.
- Some are a source of financial revenue.

12. How are targets identified? (16)
- Broadcasts on right wing radio stations
- Internet
- Print articles
- Public meetings
- The group members are not acting under the direct orders of anyone – i.e. leaders identify targets, but it is up to followers to decide what to do about them.

13. What are the group's objectives?
- To harass the target constantly. (32)
- To provoke any reaction. (43)
- To make sure the target knows he is being watched (also known as "**sensitizing**" the target). (32)
- To try and find ways of making the target interact with them (regardless of whether a target is taking the garbage out in the morning, driving to work or sitting in a local coffee shop).
- Ideally, a target will not be able to go anywhere in public without having to deal with them in some way. (37)
- To destroy a person's life by attacking the weakest point, which could include a spouse, children or elderly relatives. (47)

14. How do they achieve their objectives?
- Many tactics are tried and the result is observed. (32)
- Those which evoke a response from the target are repeated. (32)
- They discuss among themselves whether or not the target has been sensitized (i.e. made aware of the stalkers). (43)

15. How long does it last? (19)
- Most individuals remain targets for several years.
- Those involved in activism of any kind are life long targets.
- Moving will not usually help a target. If he is a target in one area, he will remain a target where ever he moves.

16. How do the groups sensitize the target?
- Picture taking (32)
- Filming (32)
- Note taking (32)
- Having uniquely marked vehicles follow the target wherever he drives, without the frequent trade-offs which are normally used. (43)
- Having that same vehicle parked in front of his house at night. (43)

17. What other tactics are used?

Vehicle-related tactics:
- Numerous different vehicles hanging around a certain area. (48)
- Traveling in convoys with highbeams on. (31)
- Drivers in convoys waving at one another. (48)
- Attempting to intercept the target's vehicle at intersections. (31)
- Trying to force the target's vehicle off the road. (48)
- Vandalizing the target's vehicle, including: (32)
  - Slashing tires
  - Scratching paint
  - Stealing license plates
  - Draining the oil or antifreeze over a period of time in the hopes of destroying the engine.
  - Removing and then returning items, putting items in the vehicles, or taking items from the residence and putting in the vehicle or vice versa.
  - They do not usually cut brake lines or commit other acts of sabotage which would leave evidence. (45)

Face-to-face tactics:
- Following a target on foot wherever he goes. (32)
- Standing around a target while he is paying for a purchase in a store. (35)
- Swarming the target – i.e. totally surrounding a target so he cannot move. (33)
- Physically intimidating a target by standing very close. (33)
- Sitting near a target in a restaurant. (35)
- Glaring at the target . (48)
- When a target sits anywhere in public, group members will attempt to sit behind him in order to create noise, by whatever means, including tapping their feet on the target's chair. (32)
- Walking by a target and doing strange things to attract his attention, such as: (37)
  - Blinking their eyes.
  - Reading the time from an imaginary watch on their wrist.
  - Making faces.

Noise Campaigns
- Generating noise around the clock. (42)
- Interfering with sleep patterns (i.e. through excessive noise). (42) Trying to wake up the target at night as many times as they can.
- Noise campaigns include:
  - People yelling and screaming outside the person's residence. (33)
  - Numerous different vehicles, squealing their tires, honking their horns and hanging around a certain area. (48)

- Apartment noise campaigns will include: (33)
  - Tapping on the walls in the middle of the night
  - Taps running
  - Hammering
  - Noises coming from the upper and/or lower apartments, and possibly the apartments on both sides
- Ideally, noises are *timed to activities of the target*, such as: (42)
  - When a target goes outside. (33)
  - When a target flushes the toilet. (37)
  - When a target turns on a water faucet. (37)
  - When a target walks near a window. (42)

Other tactics:
- Controlling the target's time, including: (42)
  - Speeding across town in a convoy of vehicles so group members can stand in line ahead of a target for the sole purpose of trying to keep him waiting as long as possible. (37/42)
  - Blocking a target from leaving a parking space. (42)
  - Controlling a target's speed on a highway by surrounding him with slow moving vehicles. (42/45)
  - Causing problems which force the target to solve them, like gluing his car doors shut. (45)
  - Creating a puzzle for the target to solve. The target is invited to waste his time following bogus clues and leads. (45)
- Imposing a system of rewards and punishments on a target for: (42)
  - Communicating and associating with other people.
  - Laughing at or assaulting group members.
- Causing problems with telephone services (and other utilities). (48)
- Sometimes audio bugs are installed in the residence of a target. (30)

18. More on occupying a target's time:

Turning the tables around on a group, by following one of their vehicles, for example, is precisely what they want. Chasing it is even better. If they can occupy a target's time that way, they will have a very successful day. They are on patrol. It is not possible to waste their time. As always, a target risks having criminal charges filed against him and there will be more than enough witnesses. (45)

Property must be secured, but a target cannot let a group control his time. He must also realize that he cannot control their time. (46)

19. Audio Surveillance: (30)

Groups will sometimes install audio bugs in the residence of a target. Typically, they use inexpensive bugs which broadcast on a frequency which can be monitored by other group members using scanners. Expensive bugs are reserved for high level targets.

If they do install a bug, group members will be able to listen to the target inside his home. Typically they use low power bugs, which do not broadcast very far, so they don't attract too much attention.

They will also monitor frequencies used by baby monitors, wireless intercoms, etc. If they are able to, they will also monitor cell phone conversations. Conventional scanners can be used to listen to conversations conducted on older cordless phones and 800 and 900 MHz. cell phones. Digital scanners are available from Canada and Mexico which can be used to eavesdrop on the conversations of newer cell phones. Only one side of the conversation is heard on a frequency. New cell phones change their broadcast frequencies frequently, which leaves gaps in the conversation, for those who are listening.

20. Some Important Points:

- The primary targets of all these tactics are the group members, not the target. The group members are the ones who are programmed. Group leaders define reality for their members, so *it doesn't matter if tactics do not work on a target.*
- *Group members are sensitized to all the tactics they employ.* (42)
- Stalking various targets is only part of the activity of these groups. Members are trained to perform a variety of activities *without question.* They do not know the objectives of their leaders. (51)
- Those targeted for harassment will have no problem concluding that someone is after them, but *most never know who it is.* (43)

21. What about the Police?

- Groups have no respect for the law or for those who enforce it. (45)
- They consider themselves to be superior to the Police, partially because of the crimes they get away with. (45)
- Groups take pride that they never quit. Actually, they do, but it takes a long intensive effort by the Police. (45)
- In small towns, the number of members in these groups can easily exceed the number of Police officers. (48)
- Groups claim that they have the support of some Police officers. If so, it is not many. (50)
- Most Police officers, except those in the South, are not familiar with the way groups operate. (50)
- In general, the Police will not talk about stalking groups. (48)
- One officer did say that there is a storm brewing as groups become larger and more numerous. (48)
- When approaching the police, it is necessary to speak with officers who handle extremist groups. (50)

22. The Use of "Coercive Persuasion" to control cult members

Coercion is defined as, "to restrain or constrain by force...". Legally it often implies the use of physical force, or physical or legal threat. This traditional concept of coercion is far better understood than the technological concepts of "coercive persuasion" which are *effective restraining, impairing, or compelling through the gradual application of psychological forces.* (37)

Over time, coercive persuasion, a psychological force akin in some ways to our legal concepts of undue influence, can be even more effective than pain, torture, drugs, and use of physical force and legal threats. (38)

With coercive persuasion you can change people's attitudes without their knowledge and volition. (38)

The advances in the extreme anxiety and emotional stress production technologies found in coercive persuasion supersede old style coercion that focuses on pain, torture, drugs, or threat in that these older systems do not change attitude so that subjects follow orders "willingly." Coercive persuasion changes both attitude *and* behavior, not just behavior. (38)

Coercive persuasion, or thought reform as it is also known, is best understood as a coordinated system of graduated coercive influence and behavior controls designed to deceptively and surreptitiously manipulate and influence individuals, usually in a group setting, in order for the originators of the program to profit in some way, normally *financially or politically.* (38)

Using *rewards and punishments,* efforts are made to establish considerable control over a person's social environment, time, and sources of social support. Social isolation is promoted. (38)

Non-physical punishments are used to create *strong aversive emotional arousals*, such as: (39)
- intense humiliation
- loss of privilege
- social isolation
- social status changes
- intense guilt
- anxiety
- manipulation

23. Internet Newsgroups/Forums:

There are Internet newsgroups which cater to stalking victims. *These groups are heavily populated with members of extremist groups. They pose as victims.* Their posts relate to the latest hi-tech weapons, and information about how they are being used against them. A victim should not confide in the people in these groups because the information they provide will be used to enhance the attack against them. (50)

24. U.S. Department of Justice defines "Vengeance/Terrorism Stalking" (53)

The following definition is taken from Chapter 22 in the 1999 *National Victim Assistance Academy Text.* The complete volume is available at the Department of Justice website (www.usdoj.gov): http://www.ojp.gov/ovc/assist/nvaa99/chap21-2.htm

Chapter 21 Special Topics
Section 2, Stalking

Categories of Stalking:

VENGEANCE/TERRORISM STALKING

The final stalking category is fundamentally different from the other three. Vengeance stalkers *do not* seek a personal relationship with their targets. Rather, vengeance/terrorist stalkers attempt to elicit a particular response or a change of behavior from their victims. When vengeance is their prime motive, stalkers seek only to punish their victims for some wrong they perceive the victim has visited upon them. In other words, they use stalking as a means to "get even" with their enemies.

The most common scenario in this category involves employees who stalk employers after being fired from their job. Invariably, the employee believes that their dismissal was unjustified and that their employer or supervisor was responsible for unjust treatment. One bizarre variation on this pattern is the case of a scout master who was dismissed for inappropriate conduct and subsequently decided to stalk his *entire* former scout troop - scouts and scout leaders alike.

A second type of vengeance or terrorist stalker, the political stalker, has motivations that parallel those of more traditional terrorists. That is, stalking is a weapon of terror used to accomplish a political agenda. Utilizing the threat of violence to force the stalking target to engage in or refrain from engaging in particular activity. For example, most prosecutions in this stalking category have been against anti-abortionists who stalk doctors in an attempt to discourage the performance of abortions.

This FAQ is posted online at:

http://www.CatchCanada.org/organizedstalking.htm

APPENDIX FOUR

Quotes from David Lawson's *Terrorist Stalking in America*

Cause Stalking is one of the tactics used by these groups to intimidate their adversaries. The primary characteristic of cause stalking is that it is done by large groups of people. A target will always be followed, but he is unlikely to see the same stalkers very often.

There are a variety of types of stalking, including casual acquaintance stalking, stranger stalking, celebrity stalking, stalking of juveniles, revenge stalking, electronic stalking, serial stalking, intimate partner stalking and cause stalking. Of all these types, cause stalking affects the smallest number of victims but involves the largest number of stalkers. Many of these groups include hundreds of people.

Cause stalking has been used by extremist groups since the early 1990s. The basic system is alleged to have been developed by the Ku Klux Klan and refined through years of use.

The number of extremist groups across the country and the number of their supporters is small by comparison to the overall population, but it is growing, particularly in rural areas. These groups have appeal to those who have feelings of inferiority, powerlessness and anger.

Groups do not just stalk individuals. They employ organized programs of harassment which include break-ins, property damage, assault and occasionally, even death. The children of a target are a favorite. One extremist leader told me that his group could do whatever a target can do and go wherever he goes. "We will do anything to achieve our objective," he said.

Groups are well financed. They can afford to rent property wherever the target lives. If he drives across the country, he will be followed by supporters of similar groups in that area. If he travels by plane, group members will meet him wherever he lands. They may even accompany him on a plane if they know his travel plan, and there is a good chance that they do.

Recruits tend to be blue collar workers who are at the bottom end of the job scale. They are janitors in apartments, hotels, etc., who have keys to get in any locked doors. They are security guards, who can let fellow members into places where they would not normally be allowed to go. They are city workers, who can, in many cities, follow a target around all day in their vehicles or have a noisy project underway near his residence. They are taxi drivers, who are always on the road. They are cable, telephone and electric company employees who can interfere with a target's service and spend time on patrol with the group, while they are on the job.

[As well as political targets (abortion workers, whistleblowers, etc.),] groups also attack targets of convenience. These people are selected because they are convenient targets, and not for any other reason. These include loners who tend to be more vulnerable to their harassment tactics than those with family and friends around them. Targets of convenience are used for practice.

Groups across the country are large enough to target those of minor importance and even those who might potentially be important. Those targeted for harassment will have no problem concluding that someone is after them, but most never know who it is. When [stalking] groups move into a neighborhood, there is an increase in the number of break-ins, noise, and it will become a high traffic area.

In a typical apartment setting, they will attempt to lease, sublet, or otherwise have access to apartments above, below, and on both sides of the target. Group members maintain a vigil around the target's residence. Surveillance on a residence is by triangulation. They watch it from three different positions. Surveillance is conducted 24 hours a day, 7 days a week.

Groups begin their operations with a "sensitization" program.

If they have occupied apartments surrounding a target, typically normal noises like toilets flushing, doors closing, people talking, etc. will not be heard. The only noises that will be heard are in response to something the target does. If he flushes a toilet, he may hear a car horn honk, the sound of a power tool or hammering, for example.

Typically, harassment tactics are not used unless a target is alone. If he is with others, group members will still surround him, but they will not reveal their presence. Many targets never experience the kind of harassment described here, because they are not alone very often. Others do not recognize that they are being harassed by an organized group. They just think that there are a lot of rude people in the world. Targets who do not experience physical harassment are still targets for other types of attacks.

A common tactic use by groups is noise campaigns. Group members will drive by the target's residence or work place, honking their horns, squealing tires, and making whatever other noise they can. They will also make noise from whatever nearby properties they have access to.

Typically, they will make noise when the target goes outside.

In an apartment setting or in a house, if they have installed listening devices, or if they can maintain a close enough presence to hear sounds coming from the target's residence, it is not uncommon for a target to hear honking horns and occasionally fire engine or ambulance sirens when he uses or flushes the toilet, or makes other noise. Targets can [also] expect to hear tapping on the walls in the middle of the night, taps running, hammering etc. from the upper and/or lower apartments, and possibly the apartments on both sides.

Group members work in shifts. They work 24 hours a day and do not take holidays. Their job is to make noise and alert the group when he leaves. They will continue to "work" on these activities for as long as they can get away with them. This activity can last for many years.

Physical harassment is used when a target has no witnesses. When a target is driving, standard practice is to surround his vehicle and attempt to control his speed. Group members also travel on roads parallel to the road being traveled by the target, in order to intercept his vehicle when he turns. [In addition,] a target will be followed on foot wherever he goes.

Sensitization tactics... are used to make sure the target knows he is being watched. Common harassment tactics used by those on foot include pen clicking, in which they repeatedly click a ball point pen, key rattling, and rattling change in their pockets while standing behind the target. Many tactics are tried and the result is observed. Those which evoke a response from the target are repeated. When a target sits anywhere in public, group members will attempt to sit behind him in order to create noise, by whatever means, including tapping their feet on the target's chair. The objective is to harass the target constantly.

Groups attempt to interfere with any business and personal relationships which the target has.

Groups are rallied by the constant "victories" they "win" in the games they play with their targets. It does not matter that the targets are not playing a game or that they even know a game is being played. Since groups are introverted, their interaction with one another is more important than their interaction with a target.

Supporters of these groups are obsessed with every aspect of their targets' lives. Whether a target is taking the garbage out in the morning, driving to work or sitting in a local coffee shop, group members try to find ways to make the target interact with them. Ideally, he will not be able to go anywhere in public without having to deal with them in some way.

Group members are taught that the target is the reason for their problems. He is the reason why their lives are a failure.

These groups are becoming larger and more numerous. While the people doing the harassing are what would be considered "losers", their tactics are no joke. Groups are well financed, they are operated as businesses, and they do have the power to destroy lives. **These [stalking] groups are cults.**

SIA information can be obtained at www.ICGtesting.com
ted in the USA
W08s1202190713

46BV00007B/115/P

9 780741 449207